GLOBAL PATHWAY

3RD EDITION

ENGLISH

DR. JERRY L. WILLIAMSON

go to NATIONS PUBLISHING

Published by Go To Nations
A division of Calvary International, Inc.

www.gotonations.org

Copyright © 2006, 2016, 2020, 2023 by Jerry L. Williamson

Global Pathway, 3rd Edition: A Leader's Guide to Building a Great Commission Church (English)
by Jerry L. Williamson
ISBN: 978-1-959735-02-1

ALL RIGHTS RESERVED
No part of this publication may be reproduced, stored in a retrieval system, or transmitted, in any form whatsoever without written permission, except where indicated. The use of short quotations or occasional page copying for personal use or group study is permitted and encouraged.

Unless otherwise indicated, Bible quotations are taken from the New American Standard Bible®, Copyright © 1960, 1962, 1963, 1968, 1971, 1972, 1973, 1975, 1977, 1995 by The Lockman Foundation. Used by permission. (www.Lockman.org); the New International Version®, NIV®, Copyright © 1973, 1978, 1984, 2011 by Biblica (formerly the International Bible Society). Used by permission of Zondervan Publishing House. All rights reserved; the King James Version®, KJV®. This translation of the Holy Bible is in the Public Domain, except for in Great Britain; the New King James Version®, Copyright © 1982 by Thomas Nelson, Inc. Used by permission. All rights reserved; and the English Standard Version, Copyright © 2001 by Crossway Bibles, a division of Good News Publishers. Used by permission. All rights reserved.

Design: Michelle Mauricio
www.trulyloved.media

Go To Nations® is a registered trademark of Calvary International, Inc. and is registered in the U.S. Patent and Trademark Office.

For information on bulk orders:

GO TO NATIONS PUBLISHING
3771 Spring Park Road
Jacksonville, FL 32207
904.398.6559

HOW TO USE THIS BOOK

This book is designed to work seamlessly with the
online course, in-person workshop, or independently.

ONLINE STUDY COURSE

Enroll in the online companion course with hours of video training that you can complete at your own pace. Visit us online at **learn.gotonations.org**

MISSION ENCOUNTER

Utilize this book at a workshop or conference. Contact us for more information or schedule a training with us at **empowerment@gotonations.org**

INDEPENDENT LEARNING

Read and study independently.

CHURCH EMPOWERMENT TOOLS

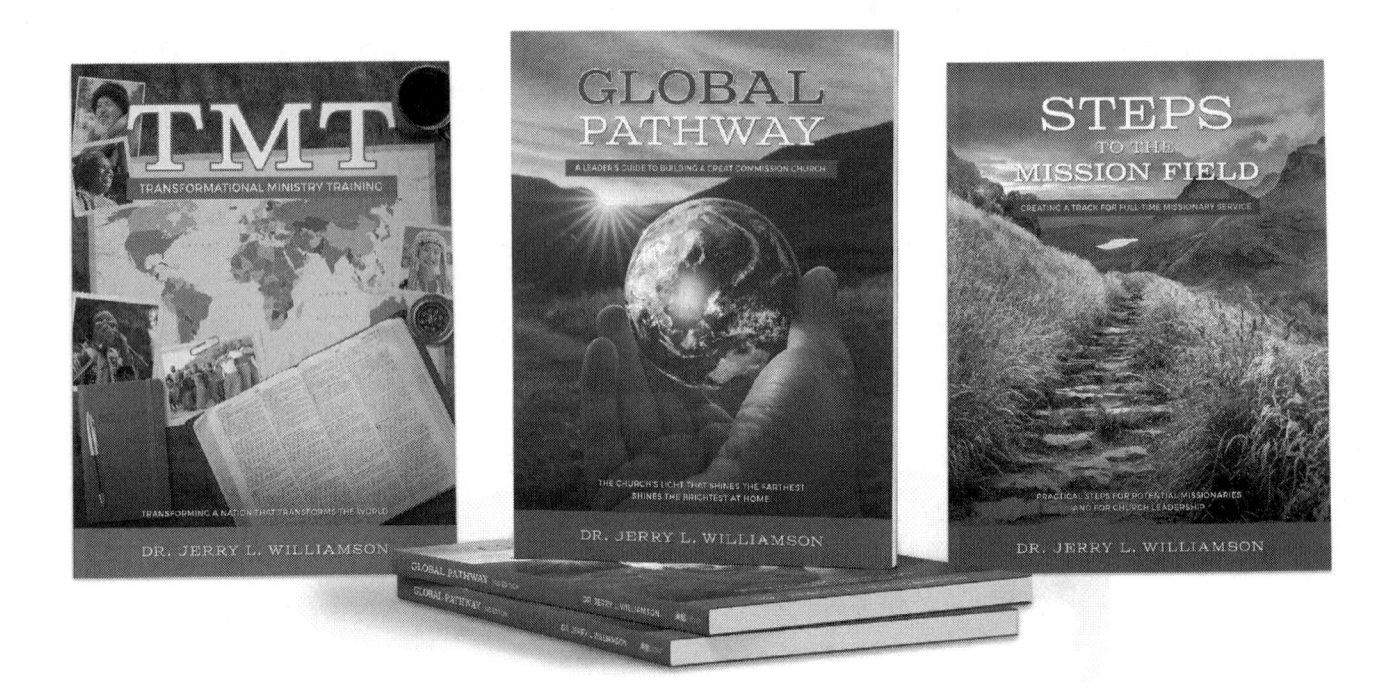

This manual is one of three Church Empowerment Training tools. By using them together as a comprehensive training package, each lays a foundation that causes the next training to be even more effective.

The 3-Part Church Empowerment Training Includes:

Transformational Ministry Training identifies seven primary areas of focus that help leaders to position the church with the proper biblical understanding to establish a national missions movement.

Global Pathway serves as a guide for church leaders concerning how to build a strong Great Commission (missions) church.

Steps to the Mission Field empowers local churches with the expertise to help people in their congregations become full-time missionaries by creating a five-stage equipping track.

When all of these training components are incorporated into the functioning operations of a church, a church network, or a denomination, it will increase their potential exponentially when it comes to their ability to impact the world through global missions.

PREFACE

It never fails to amaze me to see the heart and the drive that pastors and church leaders have for the work of God and for the welfare of the people of their congregations. They carry a dream deep within their hearts to see God's call fulfilled in their own lives and in their churches. Endless hours of work and sacrifice are often given, year after year, in order to see the church progress in true spiritual growth and purpose.

But many times, one area of the church's growth seems to fall short because the pastor does not know exactly how to approach it. The area I am talking about is the area of the church's global missions program.

After working with pastors for over thirty years in the United States and in different countries around the world, two things have become abundantly clear that we must see changed. First, pastors are operating on inadequate information when it comes to cross-cultural missions ministry. This has caused many pastors to "buy into" faulty missions concepts or to accept facts about missions that are simply not true or accurate. The result is that their churches are functioning far below their God-given missions potential.

Second, pastors can be intimidated with having to deal with the whole "missions thing," so they address the subject on a very limited basis. The congregation is left in a minimal state of understanding of missions, because it has not been made a high priority concerning the <u>purpose</u> of the church.

For the most part, church members believe in missions! They talk about how missions is some type of Christian activity, but have no real understanding how they are personally and biblically connected with it in a practical way.

Global Pathway is designed as a written step-by-step manual to empower pastors, missions directors, and church leaders to guide their congregations into a dynamic, fruitful missions ministry. They will be able to equip their church members with the scriptural and practical understanding of missions they need so they are able to embrace personally the church's missions program with faith and long-term commitment.

Global Pathway has ignited a fire for world missions in the hearts of thousands of church congregations in over thirty different nations of the world. Whether a church wants to strengthen its current missions program or launch a new one for the first time, this manual has the power to help make it happen!

ABOUT THE AUTHOR

Jerry Williamson was ordained in 1982 and served as an Associate Pastor in Missouri for three years before serving as a Go To Nations missionary in Ecuador in 1985 and 1986. In 1988, Jerry was appointed as the ministry's International Bible School Director overseeing eleven Bible schools in ten countries.

Since 1990, Jerry has served as a part of Go To Nations Executive Leadership Team and has played an active role in the planning and deployment of missions projects around the world.

Jerry created Go To Nations ten-day Missionary Preparation and Orientation (MPO) for new missionary candidates in 1991 which has drawn people from all over the world and has served as a ministry launching pad for over a thousand new missionaries into cross-cultural missions service.

He designed the initial ten-week field internship for new missionaries called the Timothy Internship Program (TIP) in 1996. This program provides the strengths of an extended, entry-level field training that addresses important areas that will help establish a solid foundation for long-term missionary service.

In June of 2000, Jerry was appointed President of Go To Nations. He oversees the Executive Leadership of the ministry and is known for his vision and direction in the global advancement of missions operations around the world.

The primary focus of Jerry's ministry is to help initiate and accelerate mission ministry on a global scale. He is well known for his zeal for missions and for his ability to articulate vision for missions with clarity.

TABLE OF CONTENTS

INTRODUCTION...xiii

THE BIBLICAL BASIS FOR MISSIONS

1. Kingdom Christianity...3

2. Great Commission Mandate...................................23

THE GREAT COMMISSION CHURCH

3. Empower the Pastor...47

    A. The Three Cs..47

    B. Ten Facts Every Pastor Should Know......................48

    - The pastor is the key to a strong missions church
    - The Church is God's instrument to reach the world
    - Any size church can have a significant role in missions
    - The church's light that shines the farthest shines the brightest at home
    - Your church can avoid horror stories concerning missions
    - The landscape of local churches is an ocean of untapped potential
    - Mega churches will not reach the world for Christ alone
    - Every church has a missionary sitting in the congregation
    - The missions program should be more than the pastor
    - Missions is a team effort

    C. Assess the Current Missions Activities..................61

4. Envision the Core..65

    Core Gathering...65

    A. Great Commission Call...................................66

    B. Great Commission Church 68

    C. Missions – Not Just Another Program 72

    D. Four Main Areas of Activation 74

    E. Missions Advancement Team 75

5. Establish a Plan 79

    A. Activate the Missions Advancement Team 79

    B. Write the Missions Plan 79

- Why create a Missions Plan?
- How do we get started?
- Missions Plan Prototype

    C. Develop Operational Procedures 82

    D. Annual Missions Calendar 82

6. Launch the Congregation 115

    A. Activate Every Part of the Church. 115

    B. Annual Missions Conference 116

- Why is it important?
- How will it benefit the Church?
- What should be accomplished?
- Main highlight of the Missions Conference
- What is a Faith Promise?
- Why should Faith Promise Giving be implemented?
- Important questions to consider
- Order of the Faith Promise Service

- The importance of Prayer
- Follow-up to the Missions Conference

    C. Maintaining your Missions Momentum 134

    D. Monthly Missions Sunday 137

    E. Short-Term Missions Trips 140

7. Implementation Process **145**

    A. Using the Quick Reference Sheet 145

    B. Action Steps – Descriptions 146

    C. Create a Missions Budget 148

APPENDIX

    Appendix A: Annual Missions Budget Worksheet 151

    Appendix B: Departmental Missions Activation Form 153

    Appendix C: Missions Conference Planner Worksheet 155

    Appendix D: Missions Conference Budget Worksheet 161

    Appendix E: Faith Promise Brochure (Text) 163

    Appendix F: Faith Promise Card (Text) 165

    Appendix G: Quick Reference Sheet 167

INTRODUCTION

The Great Commission Call

Most Christians are sitting in church totally ignorant regarding their value and how important they are in the plan of God concerning His work on the earth. Here is a simple demonstration that illustrates the condition of most believers.

Imagine three people standing side-by-side. Each of them is holding a sign that is butted end-to-end making a statement. The statement is:

Believer's / Great Commission / Call

But here is what we have done in the Church. We have made the Great Commission a special call to a chosen few. So, to demonstrate this reality, pull out the person in the center who is holding the sign that says "Great Commission." Place that person over to the side, signifying that very few are really involved with it or even really understand it.

Now look at the other two people that you left standing there with their signs. Notice the gap between the two signs that say "Believer's" and "Call." When the Great Commission is missing in someone's life, that person is disconnected from their calling. This is usually not done intentionally, but it is done out of lack of biblical training concerning the Great Commission call on the individual Christian and the Great Commission call on a church body corporately.

In the *Global Pathway* training, we will deal with how the church can restore the Great Commission in their congregation, thus reconnecting the "Believer" with their God-given "Call."

When studying church planting movements down through history, certain facts become extremely evident. For example, it is not enough to just lead people to Christ. Nor is it enough to just plant churches and build congregations of believers. That alone will not create healthy churches, nor will it sustain any type of long-term church movement.

One key component in establishing a healthy, thriving, effective church movement is *a strong focus on the Great Commission*. Any time a church is not committed to missions (meaning it is not committed to reaching out beyond its own Jerusalem), that church will eventually turn inward and become a sick church because it is the vision for missions that keeps the hearts of the congregation healthy and turned outward.

Three Core Principles

The *Global Pathway* training is based on three Core Principles. They are:

1. Every Christian is called by God to take personal ownership of the Great Commission. This deals with the *dynamic of personalization*, which means taking personal responsibility for the Great Commission to the point that it leads to a personal involvement.

2. The local church is God's primary instrument to reach the world for Christ and must be mobilized for such a purpose.

3. The local church is the seedbed for all missionaries and the sending force behind all missionaries sent to the mission field.

What *Global Pathway* is Designed to Accomplish

1. *Global Pathway* is designed to build the church's missions program on scriptural principles. Everything that we do should be based on the Bible. *Global Pathway* lays a biblical foundation for missions so the whole congregation can embrace their church's missions program with faith and confidence.

2. *Global Pathway* is designed to work in any size church. Whether the church has 25 members or 2,500 members, it doesn't matter. The principles taught will work in both situations.

3. *Global Pathway* is designed to help churches that have existing missions programs or to help churches that don't have missions programs to create new ones. Any church can benefit from the training and see their missions capabilities go to a whole new level.

4. *Global Pathway* is designed to adapt to any church's structure or government. This is extremely important! No matter what type of authority structure or decision-making process a church has in place, the principles taught in *Global Pathway* will adapt to each church's established mode of operation.

5. *Global Pathway* is designed so it does not burden the pastor with a greater on-going workload. Many pastors shy away from any type of new training because of the fear that it will simply cause more work for them. *Global Pathway* creates just the opposite. Once fully implemented, it will cause less work for the pastor with greater results.

6. *Global Pathway* is designed to activate every part of the church for the cause of completing the Great Commission. This will create a new energy and a greater sense of fulfillment in the members of the church.

7. *Global Pathway* is designed to bless the church spiritually, numerically, and financially. As each session of the training unfolds, new insight will be gained on how exactly this will happen.

Results to Expect from the *Global Pathway* Workshop

1. *Global Pathway* will provide the church with a complete and comprehensive approach to missions. We use an approach that is comprehensive but concise, with enough information to guide your process without becoming overwhelming.

2. *Global Pathway* will unify the church's congregation around a God-sized vision for global missions. The greater the purpose, the more it pulls the congregation into God's world. This reduces the influence that minor issues might normally have.

3. *Global Pathway* will allow *every* member of the church to answer their God-given Great Commission call. As pastors and leaders, we will answer to God for how we shepherded His people and prepared them for their own call.

4. *Global Pathway* will help you create a useable, written missions plan that ensures a greater impact, especially in obedience to the Great Commission and your effectiveness in engaging the global harvest.

Addressing Pastors' Concerns

When it comes to missions, pastors usually have certain concerns that need to be addressed in order to move forward with their missions programs with a sense of confidence and peace. Here are the four most common areas of concern that the training will cover:

1. Pastors' Fears—concerning the development of a missions program. *Global Pathway* eliminates land mines (blind spots) that cause most negative missions experiences.

2. Pastors' Needs—in leading a strong missions church. This training will give the pastor and his/her staff the tools to fulfill the church's vision for missions.

3. Pastors' Potential—to build a comprehensive missions program. *Global Pathway* will empower the church to establish processes that create new opportunities and capabilities for an effective missions ministry.

4. Pastors' Responsibilities—before God concerning missions as the shepherd of the congregation. This is an awesome responsibility! Without the pastor empowering his/her church in the area of missions, the members will not be equipped to fulfill their Great Commission call.

Training Process

Global Pathway is a line-by-line blueprint for building a strong Great Commission church. In other words, the teaching is progressive in nature. Each section builds upon the previous section. This is why it is critical for pastors and church leaders to follow carefully the action steps that will be presented in the training. The action steps should not be treated as a luncheon buffet. If certain components of the training are left out in its implementation, the church will see minimal results for their efforts. And here is the reason why.

The biggest problem with most church's missions programs is that they are piecemeal at best. That means their missions programs have too many missing components to be effective. *Global Pathway* gives the church a comprehensive approach to missions by implementing the missing pieces that are holding back the church's missions effectiveness.

Main Training Components

The *Global Pathway* training is divided up as:

A. The Biblical Basis for Missions

1. Kingdom Christianity: Bringing a true perspective of the Christian life
2. Great Commission Mandate: Establishing definition for the Great Commission

B. The Great Commission Church

3. Empower the Pastor: Leading the church in the area of missions
4. Envision the Core: Taking personal ownership of the Great Commission
5. Establish a Plan: Creating a written missions plan

6. Launch the Congregation: Activate everyone in your church into a personal involvement in missions.
7. Implementation Process: Following a series of action steps to implement the *Global Pathway* training

Three-Way Empowerment

By the end of the *Global Pathway* training, pastors and church members will be empowered with what we call the Three **P**s:

1. **Principles:** You will be grounded in biblical principles by which you can guide your missions program.
2. **Processes:** You will be given established standards and systems to help you carry out your vision for missions as a unified church body.
3. **Practical Tools:** You will receive the necessary components for the church to be effective in the area of missions.

BIBLICAL BASIS FOR MISSIONS

KINGDOM CHRISTIANITY

This is not meant to be an exhaustive study on this subject but rather, the next two sessions serve as a connector to how missions pertain to every local church and their congregation.

Many times, Go To Nations is asked to speak in Bible colleges and churches on the subject of the Great Commission. However, what we have learned over the years is that until a believer in Christ truly has an understanding of **Kingdom Christianity**, people seldom will truly embrace Christ's Great Commission mandate.

To have a true perspective of the Christian life and missions, we must start by teaching people to be **Kingdom Christians** *with a* **Kingdom Mindset** *preaching a* **Kingdom-centered Gospel.**

Even in many parts of the world where the Church is established, the understanding and emphasis on the Kingdom of God need to be reestablished (or at least – reinforced) again as a scriptural underpinning of the Church. In many places in the affluent West (places like the United States), the Kingdom of God and the Church are (too often) considered to be the same thing. This is not correct.

The truth is that the Church is God's instrument to expand the Kingdom of God. In reality, what we have in global Christianity today is too much of an unproductive Ministries Mentality instead of a Kingdom Mentality.

Churches today, and the ministers that lead them, spend most of their energy and resources building great ministries as if that was the mission rather than on Kingdom expansion.

This is what creates an inward-focused church that eventually leads to a post-Christian state.

Think of this: The United States has never had more mega ministries than it has right now, but regrettably the country, as a whole, has never been "worse off" spiritually. This is because most churches (especially in the West) do not think "Kingdom." We must always remember that the goal is not to build ministries, the goal is to **complete the MISSION!**

Jesus never once told us to build the Church. He said to go and make disciples of all nations. And He would build the Church.

This graph will demonstrate what we are focusing on here:

Jesus never once told us to build the Church. He said to go and make disciples of all nations.

```
Generational              Post-Christian
 Ministry                    State
    ↑                          ↑
 Kingdom                  Post-Christian
Advancement                Tendencies
    ↑                          ↑
Great Commission            Ministry
    Focus                    Building
    ↑
Church Planting
    ↑
Leadership Training
    ↑
 Evangelism
    ↑
 Unreached
```

The gray area right up the middle is what we want to see develop with all church movements.

Every Christian movement in any country starts out primarily the same.

- The unreached is targeted with the Gospel.
- As evangelism spreads, people start coming to Christ.

- This creates the need for discipleship and for the process of raising up church leaders…
- …which eventually leads to church planting.

As the church movement forms and grows…

- It is critical that it maintains a "Great Commission focus."
- This will cause on-going "Kingdom advancement."
- And that will develop into "generational ministry."

But sad to say, most new churches planted do not end up this way.

- But when a church movement grows to a certain size…
- It has a tendency to veer off course.

When a church movement grows to a certain size…

- It can lose its Great Commission focus and starts putting the majority of its time, energy and resources toward the ministries they have already established.
- Then, the focus is not about Kingdom advancement, but rather, about building and maintaining their ministry.
- At this state the fires of evangelism die. All energy and all focus are now all about quality of preservation.

Steve Smith who was a longtime church planter contended that the Church in the United States will never truly be on target until it possesses the right perspective concerning the Kingdom of God. In an article titled "Getting Kingdom Right to Get Church Right," he made this statement:

> Jesus was launching a kingdom so radical in nature that we must realign our whole concept of what God wants to do in and through us, especially in how He will do it. This includes how we live as church… Disciples throughout history have made it their priority to see the Kingdom explode among lost

It is critical that the Church maintains a "Great Commission focus."

populations; they have often seen churches multiply rapidly generation by generation through ordinary new believers.

Unfortunately, as churches become established, a tendency emerges to consolidate efforts and focus more on the church development than on Kingdom expansion.

When we begin to talk about this a natural question arises. Which priority is right? Kingdom first or church first? The answer is that both are important. However, to get church right, we must get Kingdom right first!

To be honest, having a Kingdom mindset is difficult for most Christians. Primarily, because of the majority of governmental concepts we are familiar with. For example, people in the United States, along with many other nations, have a democracy mindset instead of a Kingdom mindset. This is one of the reasons many people who claim to be Christians see nothing wrong with passing laws legalizing actions in their nation that go directly against Scripture.

Even though they claim such actions go against their own personal convictions. Their thought process is that in any democratic nation the majority of people should allow things for the sake of the convictions of the few. In holding to this belief, however, they end up voting for, and upholding, certain immoral actions that they claim go against their personal Christian beliefs.

How could an alarming portion of Christians in the so-called "Christianized West," especially the younger generation, end up with this type of thinking? The answer to such a question is the result of Christians having a democracy mindset rather than a Kingdom perspective of the Christian walk. Even more tragic is the reality that this is the mindset that is often exported overseas to other cultures.

In the light of being sensitive, thoughtful, and tolerant in such democratic nations, a large portion of the Church is putting

To get church right, we must get Kingdom right first!

most of its focus on trying to be relevant to their present culture. Certainly, all of us can understand the desire to contextualize the Gospel and to be as relevant to our surrounding culture; however, <u>cultural relativity is not our problem. Spiritual relativity is our problem!</u>

It is time that the Church quit trying to get the world to like them and accept them.

We have literally seen that instead of winning our generation to Christ we have allowed this generation to re-create Christianity into a self-actualization, self-fulfillment, feel good religion that has little impact on society.

Francis J. Pratt: US Center for World Mission (Frontier Ventures) addresses this issue by giving an explanation of how Christians have been "culturalized" rather than being an impacting force within the culture. He explains:

> The most significant problems for the Church originate in our becoming lost in earthly cultures. The net effect is that we attribute our cultures' values and beliefs to God and, in essence, reinvent God in our own image. This process has changed our reading of the Bible, our understanding of the gospel and our perception of our place in the world as the Church and our duties as the children of God.

We desperately need to re-establish a Kingdom culture in the Church. We also need to establish a Kingdom culture anywhere we carry the Gospel to other nations.

Definition of the Kingdom of God:

Before we go any further let us define the term Kingdom of God. Simply put: The Kingdom of God is any place where there is the reign of God. Every time someone accepts Jesus Christ as their Lord and Savior, the Kingdom of God is expanded.

Kingdom Christianity

Jesus' whole earthly ministry was centered around "kingdom." Everywhere He went, His message was:

"The kingdom of heaven is like a man who sowed good seed in his field…" Matthew 13:24

"The kingdom of heaven is like a mustard seed…" Matthew 13:31

"For the kingdom of heaven is like a landowner who went out early…" Matthew 20:1

"For the kingdom of heaven is like a man traveling to a far country…" Matthew 25:14

As a matter of fact, Jesus used the word "kingdom" over one hundred times and only used the word "church" twice. By doing so, He was not down-playing the importance of the Church. He was simply establishing how important it is for the Church to stay focused on Kingdom expansion, not just ministry building.

There are hundreds of books written on the Kingdom of God. Many wiser and more educated people than myself have written volumes on this subject. Though we cannot do a comprehensive study on the Kingdom of God here, we can at least understand a little about the Kingdom in order to assist us in our understanding of God's focus and thus what our focus ought to be.

Jesus began His public ministry by focusing on the Kingdom of God.

> Now after that John was put in prison, Jesus came into Galilee, preaching the gospel of the kingdom of God, And saying, The time is fulfilled, and the kingdom of God is at hand: repent ye, and believe the gospel. *Mark 1:14-15* (KJV)

Let's break this down and look at it a little more closely.

Jesus said, The kingdom is "at hand," literally meaning that, "the time has come. The Kingdom has arrived!" "The Kingdom of Heaven has just invaded earth." "I am here and I have come to represent the Kingdom."

Jesus used the word "kingdom" over one hundred times and only used the word "church" twice.

However, Jesus realized that the people of His day had a wrong perception when it came to the Kingdom of God. They had false expectations regarding the arrival of the King and His Kingdom.

Knowing that the Jewish people had these incorrect messianic expectations, Jesus announces the arrival of the Kingdom on the earth, and then, He tells them to repent and believe the Gospel. Yes, repent from your sins and come to Jesus. We understand this clearly now. But to the hearers of Jesus' words, this was a radical statement. Was there perhaps more to this "repent" statement?

Repent comes from the Greek word "metanoia" which means to change your mind, to think differently, to reconsider. Though Jesus was speaking to the Jewish people, the "chosen people of God," He boldly proclaimed that they needed to repent.

A righteousness-by-the-law type of understanding was coming to an end. The separation between God and mankind was going to be obliterated. A new day has dawned! The King has arrived and the Kingdom of God is now accessible. So, you need to REPENT, meaning you need to change the way you think about Kingdom.

Jesus was telling the Jewish people to set aside their preconceived notions that their Messiah was coming to break the power of the Roman Empire and to set up some type of earthly kingdom. Because Jesus did not come to set up an earthly kingdom, but rather a spiritual kingdom. His Kingdom was not to be, and will never be, measured by territorial borders. His Kingdom is established in the hearts of men and women as they agree and pledge allegiance to the King and to His Kinship.

A Dual Reality Regarding the Kingdom of God:

When it comes to the Kingdom, there is a dual reality that our minds have trouble comprehending.

The King has arrived and the Kingdom of God is now accessible.

In Luke 17:21 Jesus declares that, "the Kingdom of God is <u>within</u> you." Yet in other Scriptures, such as Colossians 1:13, it declares that we have been..."translated (conveyed) <u>into</u> the Kingdom of the Son of His love." The NIV translates this as, "brought us into the Kingdom."

The Kingdom of God is <u>within</u> you.

> ...giving joyful thanks to the Father, who has qualified you to share in the inheritance of his holy people in the kingdom of light. For he has rescued us from the dominion of darkness and ***brought us into the kingdom*** of the Son he loves, in whom we have redemption, the forgiveness of sins. *Colossians 1:12-14*

This is a dual reality that we must accept. Jesus, being the King of God's Kingdom, resides in us once we accept Him as Lord and Savior of our lives. There is no Kingdom without a King and this King lives in us. (John 14:23; John 17; Eph. 4:4–6; Rev. 3:20)

Understanding this dual reality of the Kingdom leads into what Jesus said in Matthew 11:12.

> And from the days of John the Baptist until now the Kingdom of heaven suffereth violence, and the violent take it by force. (KJV)

Who are these violent ones that Jesus is talking about? And what exactly are they taking by force? These violent ones are God's Kingdom people who have been translated into His Kingdom and are taking the realities of the Kingdom and making them real here on earth, thus advancing the Kingdom.

The NIV states it this way:

> From the days of John the Baptist until now, the kingdom of heaven has been forcefully advancing (*in the earth*), and (*or because*) forceful men lay hold of it (*the kingdom*). *Matthew 11:12*

For even a greater clarification and confirmation of this interpretation we turn to Luke's gospel.

> The law and the prophets were until John. Since that time the kingdom of God has been preached, and everyone is pressing into it. *Luke 16:16* (NKJV)

The violent ones are God's Kingdom people who understand and have taken hold of the Kingdom. They are now advancing on the earth, by the supernatural power of the Gospel, to invade darkness and claim the souls of men for the Kingdom.

The Kingdom of God is advancing through His Church until God has Kingdom representation in every tribe, tongue, people, and nation.

As Jesus declared,

> And this gospel of the kingdom shall be preached in all the world for a witness unto all nations; and then shall the end come. *Matthew 24:14* (KJV)

In other words, our mission, or our goal, as Christians is to expand the Kingdom to all nations (*ethnos* – people groups).

For Jesus declares in Matthew 24:14 that when the Church gets this one task accomplished, then the end shall come.

So, if we take this to its ultimate conclusion, it leads us to what all true followers of the King of kings desire to see.

> After this, I beheld, and lo, a great multitude, which no man could number, of all nations, and kindreds, and people, and tongues, stood before the throne, and before the Lamb, clothed with white robes, and palms in their hands. *Revelation 7:9* (KJV)

The Kingdom of God is advancing through His Church until God has Kingdom representation in every tribe, tongue, people, and nation.

Here is what all Christians need to realize: Kingdom expansion is our mission. The Church is God's primary instrument to carry out that mission.

God has a mission, and the Church, with all the members, are to be about that mission.

As Stephen Bevans has said, "In many respects, the church does not so much have a mission as the mission has a church."

The point is, it doesn't matter how many people we can pile in a church building if at the end of the day, the Kingdom of God has not advanced in the earth.

The Kingdom of God's Stability

Let's continue this study of the Kingdom of God with a look at its stability.

In Matthew 16:18, Jesus said, "...and the gates of hell will not prevail against the church." When reading this we need to seriously think about what the Lord was referring to. Will not prevail against the church in doing what? Build impressive ministries? NO! A thousand times, no!

Jesus is saying here that the gates of hell, Hades, the abode of the ungodly, the realm of the power of Satan, the place of torment, **will not prevail** in stopping the Church from advancing the Kingdom of God in the earth.

Kingdom people will, and are, advancing the Kingdom of God on the earth by the supernatural power of the Gospel, invading darkness and claiming the souls of men for the Kingdom. We are plundering hell to populate heaven. Kicking doors down and rescuing souls.

However, we must realize that at the same time the devil will help build great ministries if that ministry will forget about advancing the Kingdom around the world. In all seriousness, the devil doesn't care how many people we can gather in our ministry, he will even send people to your church and ministry, if you are doing little or nothing to advance the Kingdom of God around the world.

Kingdom of God as Our Life Focus

According to Jesus, what should be the life focus of a Christian? Jesus provides the answer for all of us to read in Matthew 6:33.

> But seek ye first the kingdom of God, and his righteousness; and all these things shall be added unto you. (KJV)

The very thing that Jesus told us to seek first in this life, most Christians know nothing about. Regrettably, the truth is that most Christians live Matthew 6:33 backwards. They spend all their time and energy trying to deal with "all these things," and if they have any time, energy, or resources left over they may consider doing something for the Kingdom. I believe this is the very reason why so many Christians struggle in life.

It is time to get Kingdom right! In doing so, the rest of the things in our lives will start falling into their proper places.

Kingdom of God as Our Prayer Focus

According to the Gospels, how did Jesus teach us to pray? Jesus' words to His disciples are the same to us today.

> "Thy kingdom come. Thy will be done in earth, as it is in heaven." *Matthew 6:10* (KJV)

The instruction and example prayer are clear. Jesus desires us to pray that the Kingdom of God would come forth on the earth so the will of God would take place here as it is in heaven. In essence, Jesus taught His disciples, and teaches us, that our prayer life should be focused on the advancement of His Kingdom.

The very thing that Jesus told us to seek first in this life, most Christians know nothing about.

Here is a key reality for Kingdom Christians. We are to carry out our lives focused on two main things. First, we pledge our lives to the King of the Kingdom and secondly, we expand the King's Kingdom on the earth.

Kingdom of God in The Old Testament shadows

An Old Testament "type and shadow" of this understanding of the Kingdom of God would be King David and his mighty men.

There are two accounts of David's mighty men in the Old Testament. One is found in 2 Samuel 23:8-39 and the other in 1 Chronicles 11:10-47. Anyone reading both of the accounts will have a complete picture of the valiant men who fought at David's side. While reading these passages, consider the word kingship and how kingdom works.

1 Chronicles 11:10-47 account begins by telling us that these mighty men, together with all Israel, gave David's kingship strong support to expand it over the whole land. We, as Christians, also have a king, King Jesus, and we are to give His kingship strong support to expand His Kingdom throughout the world. God gave Israel a limited territory they were to occupy. Jesus said that we are to make disciples of all nations. Therefore, our territory is the world and our assignment as ambassadors of the King is to expand our King's Kingdom to the whole world encompassing every tribe, tongue, people group, and nation.

This understanding extends to all Christians where ever they find themselves serving the King. If one is a pastor then that pastor ought not to spend all of their time and efforts building "their ministry." A pastor is to pour his/her life into raising up disciples for Christ who possess a Kingdom focus and are given the opportunity to be involved in Kingdom expansion on a local and global scale.

If someone is a business person, they are to give their best to succeed in business so they can use their influence and resources

A pastor is to pour his/her life into raising up disciples for Christ who possess a Kingdom focus and are given the opportunity to be involved in Kingdom expansion on a local and global scale.

to help perpetuate the Kingdom of God on the earth. This is living with a Kingdom mindset and focus. Our lives are to be in service of the King and His Kingdom, not focused on our own well-being and advancement.

A principle passage that every Kingdom-focused Christian must live by is found in 2 Corinthians 5:14 and 15,

> For the love of Christ compels us, because we judge thus: that if One died for all, then all died; and He died for all, that those who live should live no longer for themselves, but for Him who died for them and rose again. (NKJV)

When people catch hold of a Kingdom perspective for their lives, it totally changes the way they think about everything. As an example, I was ministering in the Philippines to a small group of businesspeople. After I had finished speaking, a lady approached me and shared that after hearing what I said, she realized that she was looking at life as a Christian all wrong.

She went on to say that she was a successful businesswoman who owned two restaurants. And because now she had plenty of money to live a nice, comfortable life, she planned to simply sit back, enjoy life, and live off what she had created.

But that morning, this businesswoman caught hold of the gospel of the Kingdom! She literally said to me, "What am I thinking? I can't sit back and simply take it easy because I can. God has given me the ability to create businesses. And now I know why. It is to help advance His Kingdom. I have the ability to do more—a lot more—but I didn't have a reason to use my business skills to do more. Now I do. I am going to start six more restaurants so I will have the ability to give more to the work of God and do my part in helping advance His Kingdom on the earth."

In Myles Munroe's book entitled *Rediscovering the Kingdom*, Myles makes this statement,

When people catch hold of a Kingdom perspective for their lives, it totally changes the way they think about everything.

The kingdom concept was born in the heart of man, placed there by his Creator as the purpose for which he was created. Despite the fact that there are many types of kingdoms throughout history, there are certain characteristics common to all kingdoms. The kingdom of God, according to Jesus, also possesses these components. Here are some you will need to know in order to understand how kingdom works:

All kingdoms have:

- A King and Lord—a sovereign
- A territory—a domain
- A constitution—a royal covenant
- A citizenry—community of subjects
- Law—acceptable principles
- Privileges—rights and benefits
- A code of ethics—acceptable lifestyles and conduct
- An army—security
- A commonwealth—economic security
- A social culture—protocol and procedures

As Christians we must understand that we are citizens of the Kingdom of God, first and foremost! The challenge to this statement often comes from citing Romans 13:1–5, with the objection that the Bible instructs us to obey the laws of the land.

1. Let every soul be subject to the governing authorities. For there is no authority except from God, and the authorities that exist are appointed by God.
2. Therefore whoever resists the authority resists the ordinance of God, and those who resist will bring judgment on themselves.
3. For rulers are not a terror to good works, but to evil. Do you want to be unafraid of the authority? Do what is good, and you will have praise from the same.
4. For he is God's minister to you for good. But if you do evil, be afraid; for he does not bear the sword in vain; for

As Christians we must understand that we are citizens of the Kingdom of God, first and foremost!

he is God's minister, an avenger to execute wrath on him who practices evil.
5. Therefore you must be subject, not only because of wrath but also for conscience' sake. *Romans 13:1–5* (NKJV)

Certainly, the Christian is to follow the laws of the land as instructed here in Romans by the Apostle Paul, up to a point. That point is when the laws of the land violate God's law.

We submit to the authority, rule, and precepts of the Kingdom of God, which are laid out for our benefit in His Word.

Kingdom believers should live a Christian life that looks radically different from that of the world. Regrettably, this is not the case for the typical church-goer-Christian. Most people within the Christian community seem to plan and conduct their lives off the same basic template as the world.

People in general, especially in more affluent countries like the United States, frame their lives around four main life-planning components: Education, Career, Security, and Reward. This is a widely accepted success model that most Americans work toward. This is also the model of life that they teach their children to work toward as well. It is also the basic template that any career, guidance, or financial counselor would use to assist someone coming to them for counsel on successful living.

However, there should be a different dominant driving force beyond just these four components for the life of anyone who is a true Kingdom follower of Christ. That dominant force is our calling as Kingdom Believers!

Please do not misunderstand the emphasis here. There is nothing necessarily evil or wrong with those four components that are mentioned above as life-planning components, until they are not put in the context of a KINGDOM MINDSET. None of them standing on their own merit should be considered as an adequate plan for the life of a Kingdom Christian.

Kingdom believers should live a Christian life that looks radically different from that of the world.

The danger in following the pattern of the world with no real "Kingdom mindset" when it comes to our life, is that Christians have replaced God's desire with their own.

- Spiritual empowerment has been replaced with an education.
- Our God-given mission has been replaced with a career.
- Faith in Christ has been replaced with a false sense of worldly security.
- God's eternal promises have been replaced with temporal earthly rewards.
- And when you add it all up, it equals trading in the Great Commission for the American dream.

The American dream may have started out as a symbol of hope to many, but it has morphed into a pursuit of self-advancement, self-esteem, and self-sufficiency through individualism, materialism, and universalism. In the process of pursuing this idealistic life, many have lost the reality of their purpose as ambassadors of the King and His Kingdom.

The Ultimate Threat to the Kingdom of God

The ultimate threat to the advancement of the Kingdom of God is not the misguided people in the world that are doing everything possible to destroy Christianity. Nor is it the devil. He is a defeated foe and should be treated as such. The greatest threat to the advancement of the Kingdom is the Christians themselves getting caught up with simply living life.

Sadly, many Christians have simply disengaged from what God called them to be and to do concerning the Kingdom. Life takes over, and their Christian walk becomes more of a moral discipline in a secular context rather than a destiny to fulfill during their time on earth. The Apostle Paul warned Timothy that it is the "affairs of this life" (2 Timothy 2:4) that represent the greatest danger to the Church and the mission of the Kingdom.

The greatest threat to the advancement of the Kingdom is the Christians themselves getting caught up with simply living life.

Paul gives us this instruction:

> No soldier in active service entangles himself in the affairs of everyday life, so that he may please the one who enlisted him as a soldier. *2 Timothy 2:4 (NASB)*

This Scripture paints an incredible picture pertaining to us as Kingdom believers. We are the army of God! We represent the Kingdom of God on the earth. We have received our marching orders from our Commander in Chief, the Lord Jesus Christ. When we know this, it is critical that we do not allow the affairs or the circumstances of life to stop us from carrying out our Great Commission mandate.

A Kingdom-Centered Gospel

If we are going to be effective ministers that produce lasting fruit, we must be preaching a Kingdom-centered Gospel. This was the only kind of Gospel that Jesus preached. It is also the Gospel message that Jesus instructed for us to preach. However, in the USA, we focus almost entirely on preaching a gospel of salvation, not the gospel of the Kingdom.

Jesus never preached publicly one time on salvation. Jesus spoke about being born-again one time to one man, Nicodemus, at around 2:00 a.m. There is a big difference between preaching the gospel of salvation and the gospel of the Kingdom of God. Salvation is important. Salvation is the door into the Kingdom. But it is only a part of the Gospel message.

Pastor Bill Johnson addresses this differentiation this way,

> The gospel of salvation is glorious, but it is just a part of the gospel of the Kingdom. The gospel of salvation is focused on *going* to heaven. The gospel of the Kingdom is focused on *bringing* heaven. We have to stop confusing our destination with our assignment.

When a person's understanding of the Gospel is limited only to salvation and his total focus is simply on getting to heaven, the Great Commission mandate is lost in the process. Under this understanding, Christians simply focus their lives on being good providers for their families and being good church members for their communities. While the very reason we are on this planet is negated.

The average Christian thinks that the Great Commission is an extra-curricular program in the Church. The conclusion, therefore, is that missions is a special call to a chosen few and Christians default into a belief that becoming scripturally mature in all of the topics attached to the circle below is the mission in life. They do not understand that all Christians are to "grow up" in these areas so that they are able to focus on the real mission, the Great Commission of our King.

The average Christian thinks that the Great Commission is an extra-curricular program in the Church.

```
         Prayer
   Serving      Giving
 Love    MISSION   Marriage
  Children       Family
         Worship
```

In my book, *The Pulse of a Nation,* I gave this example,

> While I was preaching in a church recently, I made this statement: "This might be a shock to some of you, but having a good marriage is not your mission in life; nor is just raising good children your mission in life." I could tell that the people were surprised I would say that, and that tells us something about where most Christians are at spiritually today.

The truth is we are to become strong in our marriages, in our families, and in all the areas that the Bible teaches, so we can get past all of our personal "issues" and apply more of our energy toward the real mission.

The Church serves as God's instrument to train Christians to be strong in every area of life so they are equipped to avoid becoming entangled with the affairs of this life. If a person's life consists of all the problems (issues) they can handle, they end up never getting to the Great Commission. God wants us to "grow up" in Him to the point that the circumstances of life no longer dominate us so we can focus on getting the real mission completed.

John Piper pleads with the body of Christ with these words,

> We are aliens, and living like aliens is utterly necessary. When professing Christian aliens are absorbed into the world and give up walking by the constitution of the Kingdom, and give up loving the King, and give up pursuing the cravings of the Kingdom, then they have no warrant for thinking that they will inherit the Kingdom. It is a great tragedy when a professing believer lives for this present world.

As this discussion closes, let us reread what Steve Smith said,

*Let's get Kingdom right
so we can get Church right.*

Scripture paints an incredible picture pertaining to us as Kingdom believers. We are the servants of our King and have been commissioned to expand our King's Kingdom.

Let us daily pray as Jesus taught us to pray **May God's Kingdom come forth in the earth so that His will be accomplished here as it is in heaven.**

God wants us to "grow up" in Him to the point that the circumstances of life no longer dominate us so we can focus on getting the real mission completed.

Kingdom Christianity
Discussion Questions:

Did this session spark something that you had not considered?

What does this statement mean to you?

*"Cultural relativity is not our problem.
Spiritual relativity is our problem!"*

THE GREAT COMMISSION MANDATE

2

The purpose of this chapter is to bring a biblical understanding of what the Great Commission is, to whom it is given, and the challenge that is before us.

To help lay a biblical foundation for the Great Commission, I believe it is important to understand (what I call) the spiritual framework of the Christian life.

When we study the early Church's doctrine, the first thing we realize is that it was extremely simple. Especially when we compare it to all the different doctrines, Statements of Faith, and ordinances we have today in the Church at large. The early Church's doctrine was built around two central pieces: The Great Commandment and the Great Commission. In some cases, we need to recapture and re-establish this criteria today concerning the FOCUS of the Church.

In Matthew 22:36-40 we read of a lawyer of the Jewish law who came to Jesus and asked, "Master, which is the great commandment in the law? Jesus said unto him, Thou shalt love the Lord thy God with all thy heart, and with all thy soul, and with all thy mind. This is the first and great commandment. And the second is like unto it, Thou shalt love thy neighbor as thyself. On these two commandments hang all the law and the prophets." (KJV)

Let's look at some of the background to this passage. The different Jewish sects were trying to get rid of Jesus. They were taking turns trying to trick Jesus into saying something they could charge against Him and then arrest Him. Actually, the Pharisees were the main organizing group. The Herodians were the first who approached Him—with the issue of paying taxes to Caesar. Then, the Sadducees appeared—with a question about the resurrection. Then came the Pharisees—with a lawyer (expert in the law). So now, it was the Pharisees' turn—they were the legalistic bunch of the day. Therefore—<u>on purpose</u>, the lawyer's question was very specific and exact in nature. The question was: "What is <u>the</u> greatest commandment?" Jesus answered the question, "Love God with all of your heart, soul and mind." But Jesus refused to stop there. He included the second commandment as well: "Love your neighbor as yourself." In other words, Jesus refused to separate these two commandments.

Verse 40: Jesus declared, "On these two commandments hang all the law and the prophets." James called this ...***the royal law***... (James 2:8).

Here's what I want you to see. Bible theologians many times point out that loving God and loving our neighbor are so intertwined in the wording of Scripture that they are not meant to be separated. We read in 1 John 4:20-21, "If a man say, I love God, and hateth his brother, he is a liar: for he that loveth not his brother whom he hath seen, how can he love God whom he hath not seen? And this commandment have we from Him, That he who loveth God love his brother also." (KJV)

Bible theologians point out that loving God and loving our neighbor are not meant to be separated.

Catch what John said here. If you truly love God, you will <u>automatically</u> love your brother.

Understanding this statement will reveal something very important. Our lives are built on two relationships: Our relationship with God and our relationship with others (humanity).

God
↑
|
|
You ⟶ Humanity

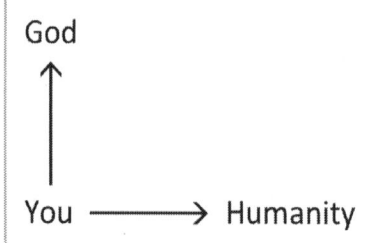

- One is a vertical relationship.
- One is a horizontal relationship.

24　Global Pathway 3rd Edition

Here is what every Christian must understand: By carrying out the first commandment (loving God) gives us the ability to fulfill the second commandment (loving humanity).

When we nurture this vertical relationship with God by spending quality time in His presence, we start taking on the nature of God. His attributes, His character, His heart, His ways, His desires, and His passions become ours. We will, literally, start acting like God and imitating God—as the Apostle Paul commands us in Ephesians 5:1, "We are to be imitators of God."

Research studies show that the average person takes on the personality, mannerisms, and habits of the five closest people in their lives. This is why it is important to be aware with whom you spend your time.

Allow me to illustrate this with a personal story. One summer when I was eight years old, I visited my uncle Bill on his huge chicken farm. Uncle Bill was a tall, slender man who always wore blue overalls. He walked with his chest sticking out and his thumbs tucked under the sides of the suspenders of the overalls. Uncle Bill had a son about my age, my cousin Kenny. I had not seen Kenny since I was about four years old, so I remembered very little about him.

When Kenny came walking out of the house to greet me, he looked like a miniature version of Uncle Bill. He was wearing blue overalls just like his dad. He even walked like his dad with his chest sticking out and his thumbs tucked under the sides of the suspenders of the overalls. It was amazing how Kenny even talked like Uncle Bill with a raspy quality to his voice. As incredible as it seemed that Kenny looked like, acted, and even sounded like his dad, it is really quite natural. Kenny spent a lot of time with his dad working on the farm. His dad was the biggest influence in his life and, overtime, he simply took on his father's attributes, characteristics, and even his disposition.

Research studies show that the average person takes on the personality, mannerisms, and habits of the five closest people in their lives.

If this is true in the natural that we take on the attributes, characteristics, and even the disposition of those we spend most of our time with; how much truer is this with God? When we spend time with God, we take on His attributes, His characteristics, and even His disposition. We take on His character, or I could say, His heart.

So, we may ask the question, "What is the heart of God?" We can find the answer to God's heart in John 3:16 and following, when we read, that "God so loved the world that He gave His only begotten Son."

When you catch the heart of God, you catch a heart for a lost and hurting world. How do we know if we are fulfilling the first commandment? The answer is simple: by seeing if we are fulfilling the second commandment.

Another way to understand this is by looking at the fruit of the first vertical relationship with God. If that relationship is not causing a heart for lost and hurting humanity, your love and devotion for God is shallow.

When you catch the heart of God, you catch a heart for a lost and hurting world.

The conclusion is that when we are living the first commandment, we will automatically carry out the second commandment.

God's Framework for a Christian's Life

```
              God
               ↑
          Our Identity
       Great Commandment
               |
                        Our Purpose
          Man ─────  Great Commission  ───→ Humanity
```

Our first relationship with God gives us our <u>identity</u>. Our second relationship with humanity exposes our <u>purpose</u>. Our first relationship is the <u>Great Commandment</u>! Our second relationship is the <u>Great Commission</u>!

As followers of Christ, we are called to have a Great Commandment – Great Commission focused life. This becomes the framework for true Christian living. This is a lifestyle of Kingdom living.

Let us now look at the true scriptural meaning of the Great Commission found in Matthew 28:19-20.

> [19] Go ye therefore, and <u>teach</u> all nations, baptizing them in the name of the Father, and of the Son, and of the Holy Ghost: [20] Teaching them to observe all things whatsoever I have commanded you: and, lo, I am with you always, even unto the end of the world. Amen.

Even though the King James version translates the Greek word "matheteuo" as <u>teach</u>, which is a correct meaning, it does not convey the complete meaning.

Though the word *mathéteuó* (math-ayt-yoo'-o) is often translated with the sense of <u>teaching in mind</u>, this only provides a partial meaning. *Mathéteuó* carries the meaning of making a pupil, a disciple, training, instructing, and teaching in order to have a total change in mind that has external results visible in a person's actions.

It is for this reason that the New King James, along with many other modern translations, translate verse 19 as, "Therefore go and <u>make disciples</u> of all nations..." This translation gives us the broader and fuller meaning behind this Greek word. Jesus is commanding, directing, and exhorting His disciples to begin the action of making disciples now and continue the making of such disciples in all nations.

Greek scholars are also quick to point out that everything described in verses 19 and 20 is pointing back to this one act of making disciples. Everything mentioned—go, baptize, teach to observe—serves as the process of making a disciple.

We are called to have a Great Commandment – Great Commission focused life.

Therefore, our central mission as believers in Christ, both individually and corporately, is to assist this process of making disciples. Where are we to make disciples? We are to make disciples in all nations! How do we make disciples in all nations? We make disciples in all nations by going, baptizing, and teaching them to observe.

The word "observe" in verse 20 is derived from the Greek word *téreó* (tay-reh'-o). It strongly emphasizes how we are to approach and treat the Great Commission. The word "observe" means to guard, to prevent from escaping. It implies a fortress, something that cannot be tore down, minimized, or lost.

Think of it this way, Jesus is telling us that we must not let anyone tear down, minimize, or lose the importance of carrying out His Great Commission mandate.

Just getting people saved does not fulfill the Great Commission alone. Bringing people to salvation is important, but it is only a part of carrying out the Great Commission. Here we can recall the quote by Pastor Bill Johnson regarding salvation and Kingdom understanding from our last chapter:

> The gospel of salvation is glorious, but it is just a part of the gospel of the Kingdom. The gospel of salvation is focused on *going* to heaven. The gospel of the Kingdom is focused on *bringing* heaven. We have to stop confusing our destination with our assignment.

If our discipleship does not impart a Christian worldview, a transformation into a Kingdom-minded disciple who understands the importance of making disciples, it is not biblical discipleship at all. There is no true discipleship without the biblical understanding and engagement of the Great Commission.

We can now both, ask and answer, the important question: "What is the definition of the Great Commission?"

Just getting people saved does not fulfill the Great Commission alone.

The Great Commission is a mandate from Christ to the Church to go and make disciples in every nation.

If a church is not involved in this local and global process, it is not a true New Testament church. Stephen Bevans echoes this sentiment in writing, "Mission therefore, is not simply one activity among many in which the church engages; it is, rather, that church's reason to exist."

Vatican II described the Church as, "missionary by its very nature." And missiologist J. Andrew Kirk, states that, "If the Church ceases to be missionary, it has not just failed in one of its tasks, it has ceased being the Church."

The reality is that the Great Commission is the purpose of the Church, not an optional or extra-curricular program in the Church. As far as Jesus is concerned, every Christian's time on this earth is to be used to help make disciples of all nations. All other details in our lives are simply a maturing and empowering process to help make that happen.

With this understanding, the Great Commission exposes our purpose as Christians. Therefore, as Kingdom believers, we live with a sense of divine purpose knowing that we have a limited amount of time (our life span) to carry out this purpose. This means that time is our most valuable possession that God has given to us. It is the one thing we cannot make more of. We can make more money, vehicles, buildings, and more of a lot of things, but we cannot make more time.

A.T. Pierson, an internationally known American (USA) pastor at the end of the 1800s, who preached over 13,000 sermons and wrote over fifty books, makes this statement about our response as Christians to Christ's Great Commission not being an option.

> Our great captain has left us His marching orders: Go ye into all the world and preach the Gospel to every creature. ...Such a plain command makes all other motives comparatively

The reality is that the Great Commission is the purpose of the Church.

unnecessary. ...Where there has been given a clear divine word of authority, immediate, implicit, submission and compliance will be yielded by loyal, loving disciples. Even to hesitate, for the sake of asking a reason, savors the essence of rebellion.

Powerful words from a spiritual giant of his time!

David Livingstone, the famous Scottish missionary who dared to venture into some of the darkest and most dangerous parts of Africa in the 1800s, opening up over one-third of the continent to the gospel, says this about the Great Commission,

> If a commission by an earthly king is considered to be an honor, how can a commission by a Heavenly King be considered a sacrifice?

Another scriptural way to explain the Great Commission is:

The Great Commission is a *command*, not a suggestion.

Evidently, the disciples believed that this was a command indeed as they were strictly warned not to speak in the name of Jesus. Acts 4:18, "And they called them and commanded them not to speak at all nor to teach in the name of Jesus." Verses 19 and 20 provide us with Peter and John's profound reply:

> But Peter and John answered and said to them, "Whether it is right in the sight of God to listen to you more than to God, you judge. For we cannot but speak the things which we have seen and heard." (NKJV)

Jesus gave us the Great Commission in all four Gospels and the Book of Acts.

- **Matthew 28:19–20,** "Go and make disciples in all nations…"

Jesus gave us the Great Commission in all four Gospels and the Book of Acts.

- **Mark 16:15,** "Go and preach the gospel to every creature..."
- **Luke 24:46–48,** "...repentance and remission of sins should be preached in his name among all nations."
- **John 17:18,** "As You sent Me into the world, I also have sent them into the world."
- **John 20:21,** "...as the Father hath sent me, even so send I you."
- **Acts 1:8,** "...but you shall receive power ... and you shall be witnesses to Me."

The reality is that once you understand God's passion for all nations to know His glory, you begin to see that the whole Bible expresses God's Great Commission mandate.

Here are just a few verses that illustrate God's heart for the nations:

- **Genesis 12:1–3,** Abram becomes the first cross-cultural missionary—Abraham means Father of a multitude—all the families of the earth shall be blessed through him.
- **1 Chronicles 16:24,** "Declare His glory among the nations, His wonders among all peoples."
- **Psalm 46:10,** "Be still, and know that I am God; I will be exalted among the nations, I will be exalted in the earth!"
- **Psalm 2:8,** "Ask of Me, and I will give you the nations for your inheritance, and the ends of the earth for your possession."
- **Psalm 96:3,** "Declare His glory among the nations, His wonders among all peoples."

Even in the Epistles we read of the Great Commission. In 1 Peter 2:9 we read, "But you are a chosen generation, a royal priesthood, a holy nation, His own special people, **that you may PROCLAIM** the praises of Him who called you out of darkness into His marvelous light." (NKJV)

The whole Bible expresses God's Great Commission mandate.

The Bible declares that we are people of proclamation! We are to proclaim the Praises of God who, in Christ Jesus, has called us out of the darkness of our sin and fleshly bondage and into His marvelous Kingdom of light. This is the Gospel. We are His people, chosen to proclaim His Kingdom Gospel to all nations.

MEASURING THE HARVEST:

When Jesus commanded us to make disciples in all nations, the word "nations" in the Greek is "ethnos." Every time Jesus used this word, it is translated as "nations" in the New Testament. In the English language we recognize this as "ethnic," as in ethnic people, ethnic food, and ethnicity.

The Bible declares that we are people of proclamation!

Some scriptural examples of the usage of this word are:

- **Matthew 24:14,** "And this gospel of the kingdom shall be preached in all the world for a witness unto all nations (ethnos); and then shall the end come."
- **Matthew 25:32,** "And before Him shall be gathered all nations (ethnos)."
- **Matthew 28:19,** "Therefore go, and make disciples in all nations (ethnos)."
- **Mark 11:17,** "Then He taught, saying to them, 'Is it not written, 'My house shall be called a house of prayer for all nations'? But you have made it a 'den of thieves.'"
- **Luke 24:47,** "...and that repentance and remission of sins should be preached in His name to all nations, beginning at Jerusalem."
- **Romans 1:5,** "Through Him we have received grace and apostleship for obedience to the faith among all nations for His name..."
- **Revelation 7:9,** "After these things I looked, and behold, a great multitude which no one could number, of all nations, tribes, peoples, and tongues, standing before the throne and before the Lamb, clothed with white robes, with palm branches in their hands..."

When Jesus used the word "nations," He was not talking about geopolitical borders like we think of nations. He was talking about distinct ethnic people groups. There are a multitude of people groups in each geopolitical nation, and it is Christ's mandate to the Church to present the Gospel to all of them.

The definition of a people group:

The late Dr. Ralph Winter, was a leading missiologist and long-time professor of missions at The School of World Mission (now known as: School of Intercultural Studies) at Fuller Theological Seminary, he defines a people group as:

> A significantly larger grouping of individuals who perceive themselves to have a common affinity for one another because of their language, religion, ethnicity, residence, occupation, class or caste situation, etc., or a combination of these.

For more information on people groups, see Dr. Ralph Winter's article entitled "The Unreached Peoples Challenge" by Ralph D. Winter and Bruce A. Koch. (http://www.missionfrontiers.org/issue/article/finishing-the-task)

Characteristics that make up a people group are things that they have in common such as:

- Common self-name
- Common identity of individuals
- Common history
- Common language
- Customs
- Family and clan identities
- Inheritance patterns
- Common ethnic factors, etc.

The clarifying and identifying different people groups in the earth, from a scriptural perspective, has been taking place for over fifty years. People like Patrick Johnstone and the late Dr.

There are a multitude of people groups in each geopolitical nation.

Ralph Winter, along with programs like the Joshua Project, have made significant contributions in this area of research.

According to the Joshua Project, the current number of people groups in the world is 17,424. The mission that our Lord Jesus gave the Church was, and still is, to make disciples among every one of these 17,424 people groups.

Most missiologists consider a group reached when there is an established replicating church movement among the group and the Christian population of that group has reached two percent. This has been accomplished among 9,500+ people groups which are now considered to be "Reached People Groups." The remaining people groups are defined as "Unreached People Groups" which number some 7,000+.

The remaining Unreached People Groups number some 7,000+.

An Unreached People Group is a people group in which less than two percent of the population are Evangelical Christians. Therefore, an Unreached People Group can be considered "a people group within which there is no indigenous community of believing Christians able to evangelize this people group."

The Unreached People Groups can be further divided into two main categories: Unengaged and Engaged. Unengaged indicates that there is no continual, on-site Christian outreach taking place to that people group. Engaged indicates that there is, presently, an on-going, on-site Christian outreach taking place toward that people group.

There is an estimated 3.05 billion people in the world who have never heard the Gospel message one time. The number of Unengaged People Groups is widely debated. It varies greatly from 600 to 3,000 based on whose data you refer to. The conclusion is that out of the 7,000+ Unreached People Groups, it is probably safe to say that 4,000 to 5,000 of them have some Christian work currently trying to reach them with the gospel. They are now being Engaged. That leaves roughly 2,000 to 3,000

Unreached People Groups that are not being engaged at this time. See www.peoplegroups.org for more information.

Where do most of these Unreached People Groups reside? The most unreached area of our planet is what is known as the 10/40 Window. This is a term coined by Christian missionary strategist Luis Bush in 1990. This imaginary window is 10 degrees north to 40 degrees north latitude above the equator. It runs across Northern Africa, the Middle East, India, China, and a portion of Southeast Asia. See illustration below.

It is in this window of fifty-nine nations that we find the majority of Unreached People Groups; ninety-seven of the least Reached People Groups on earth live within this area.

> *The most unreached area of our planet is what is known as the 10/40 Window.*

Within this 10/40 Window there are some surprising statistics that are important to note:

- 82% of the poorest of the world's poor are located in this unique area.
- 84% of those with the lowest quality of life reside in this geographic window.
- The majority of the world's unevangelized and Unreached geopolitical nations and cities are in this window.
- The hub of the world's major non–Christian religions are located in this window: Islam, Buddhism, and Hinduism.

The Most Unreached Area: The 10/40 Window

The Great Commission Mandate

Here is just a small list of countries with the most Unreached People Groups that are located in this area.

Countries	People Groups	Unreached People Groups
India	2,596	2,283
China	504	415
Pakistan	390	375
Bangladesh	402	355
Nepal	335	312
Russia	161	77

We can break down the types of Unreached People Groups (UPGs) in each nation using specific research criteria. For example, we can look at the religious groups within each country. Below is an example of Russia:

Country: Russia (77 Unreached People Groups)
- 52 Islamic
- 16 ethnic religions
- 7 Buddhists
- 1 Hindu
- 1 non-religion

When we look at the world today, thirty percent of humanity consider themselves to be Christian. This breaks down to 800 million born-again Christians with 1.37 million nominal Christians coming from a Christian culture. Finally, 1.8 billion are not yet Christian, but have the Gospel available or it is within reach of them currently. (Estimates from the Research Department of the U.S. Center for World Mission–Frontier Ventures.)

It is the Unreached People Groups who do not have access to the Gospel. It is important to understand that a person lost in the Christian world is just as lost as a person in the Unreached world; however, access to the saving message of the Gospel is what is considerably different. Both persons are equally lost but there is not equal access to the Gospel.

It is the Unreached People Groups who do not have access to the Gospel.

Often the question is asked, "Why is the Great Commission not completed?" I must make this very clear: God did His part to reach the nations. He gave His best. He sent His Son to take away our sin allowing us to reunite with the Father as His sons and daughters, and thereby, regain our rightful place as God's Regents on this earth. He is now waiting for us to do our part.

When Jesus was on the earth, He did three things concerning the Church:

1. He birthed the Church. (John 20:22; Acts 1:8)
2. He commissioned the Church. (Matthew 28:19)
3. He empowered the Church to carry out the Commission. (Acts 1:8)

Regrettably, 2,000 years later, we are still dinkin' around with the one mission He gave us to carry out and complete. Sure, there are great external hindrances that the Church must overcome to complete the Great Commission; however, the Church also has to deal with internal or self-inflicted hindrances. Let us now turn our attention to these issues. Below are four challenges that I believe must be addressed in this hour to see the Great Commission completed.

1. Spiritual Challenge

As Christians, all of us must understand that global advancement of the Gospel is "spiritual war." The enemy of God, and therefore the enemy of the Church, does not desire the advancement of the Gospel by setting in the reign of God in people's hearts. As Scripture informs us, the enemy does not come but to steal, kill, and destroy any potential seed of the Gospel. This is exemplified in the parable of the sower and the seed that Jesus shared in Matthew 13. If the enemy cannot steal or destroy, he will kill. We see this as a present-day fact around the world.

> *Regrettably, 2,000 years later, we are still dinkin' around with the one mission He gave us to carry out and complete.*

More Christians have been martyred for their faith in the 20th century than in the previous 19 centuries combined. Let that sink in for a moment. We have an enemy who desires nothing but to kill God's people and destroy the message they carry, thus destroying any potential for the Kingdom of God to have dominion in the hearts of people.

Further global advancement of the Gospel message will not be without spiritual opposition. This is warfare. The remaining Unreached areas of our world are some of the most difficult areas to reach due to the spiritual challenges that must be dealt with. Let's not kid ourselves—this is not going to be easy!

2. People Challenge

The remaining people groups are the most difficult to penetrate. Most of them are in very remote and isolated locations making it difficult to make physical contact with them. There are also great language and cultural barriers to deal with. Many of the remaining Unreached People Groups do not have any Scriptures in their language. Being so isolated, they have had very limited contact with other cultures and are, therefore, very suspicious of outsiders.

When it comes to religion, many of these people groups are religious fundamentalists, holding strong beliefs that are anti-Christian and in direct opposition to the Christian faith. Thus, making them very resistant to the Gospel that Christian missionaries would attempt to bring in.

3. Political / National Challenge

The countries with the most Unreached Peoples tend to be closed to Christianity. Continuing the isolation understanding, many of these geopolitical nations have political barriers to any religion outside their nation coming in.

Global advancement of the Gospel message will not be without spiritual opposition.

For example, Afghanistan, located practically in the middle of the 10/40 window, has 37+ million people and has only 0.1% of that population counted as Christian adherents. The country, for all intents and purposes, is a total Islamic state which has been torn by war for over thirty years. It has 48,000+ mosques, but does not have public Christian churches. It does not have any Christian radio, or bookstores, or open Christian training centers. The government of Afghanistan is an Islamic government ruling the nation under that one religion's beliefs. The constitution of Afghanistan opens with these lines:

> THE CONSTITUTION OF AFGHANISTAN
> In the name of God, Most Gracious, Most Merciful Praise be to Allah, the Cherisher and Sustainer of the Worlds; and Praise and Peace be upon Mohammad, His last Messenger and his disciples and followers.

In other words, a divergence from Islam is to deny one's country, people, family, and god, and will be dealt with in the severest of measures. This is the type of political challenge the Church of Jesus Christ must be prepared to overcome.

4. Church Challenge

An estimated ninety percent of all churches worldwide do not have viable missions programs. The direct result of this is that we currently have a global Church that is not mobilized to carry out the one task that Jesus gave us. This lack of having a viable missions program creates an imbalance in missionary distribution. Over eighty-five percent of all cross-cultural missionaries minister among nominal Christian peoples. Yet, for every one million unreached Muslims, there are fewer than three missionaries trying to reach them.

There is also an imbalance in the distribution of church finances. The United States is still considered as one of the top financers of global evangelism, but the truth is that most of this giving for missions from America (USA) is not coming from

Over eighty-five percent of all cross–cultural missionaries minister among nominal Christian peoples.

the Church's congregations, like in decades past. Congregant members who have a Great Commission mentality understand that monies given to their local church often do not reach the mission field, but rather the funds are directed toward the internal operations of that church. This has created a visible trend where finances are being directed around the local church and given directly to missions work around the world. Thus, the majority of finances for the mission movement around the world is coming from individual donors, thus circumventing the local church.

To illustrate this point, according to many different sources we continue to see that the American (USA) Church's spending consistently follows this pattern:

- 98% – Internal Church Operations
- 2% – Missions (A historic low, more was given to missions during the Great Depression)

Sources: *Empty Tomb* & *World Magazine*

A further examination of these "internal church operations," specifically regarding evangelism, finds that ninety-seven percent of all funds spent on local evangelism, by the local church, is used to target Christians. This means that churches are seeking to attract mostly other church attenders rather than reaching the unevangelized. To quote the famous radio orator, Paul Harvey, "Too many Christians are no longer fishers of men, but the keepers of the aquarium."

Ninety-seven percent of all funds spent on local evangelism, by the local church, is used to target Christians.

When it comes to wealth, we often think that it is the Muslim world that holds the most money, because we think of all Muslims as rich sultans with millions of dollars. Nothing could be further from reality. It is not the Muslims that hold the majority of the world's wealth but in fact it is the Christians that hold the largest percentage of the global wealth. According to a study done back in 2015, research shows that fifty-five percent of the total world's wealth is in the hands of Christians (USD

107,280 billion). Muslims only hold 5.8% (USD 11,335 billion) of the world's worth, Hindus hold 3.3%, and Jews hold 1.1%. (https://economictimes.indiatimes.com/news/company/corporate-trends/christians-hold-largest-percentage-of-global-wealth-report/articleshow/45886471.cms)

So, if Christians have the majority of the world's worth, and the richest countries in the world are the Christian countries, why do we not see a greater advancement of the Christian faith versus the worldwide advancement of the Islamic faith? The biggest difference between the Muslims and the Christian world Church, is that the Muslims are intentionally investing a majority of their money on the advancement of Islam globally. They have a profound financial connection with their ideological principles to make every nation an Islamic nation. They use their wealth to infiltrate poor countries by providing financial relief in order to see their religious desires advance and take hold in that country.

This is not the case when it pertains to the way the American (USA) Church or other Christian nations view their resources. Christians do not have the same level of profound financial connection regarding the advancement of the Kingdom of God globally. This is not just detrimental to world evangelism; it is detrimental to our churches as well. Robert Wilder, made this statement almost a century ago:

> The hope of the church is missions! It is not simply how we shall save the world, but how we shall save ourselves. The church that forgets the world will speedily be forsaken of the Holy Spirit.

J. Ross Stevenson stated that:

> The non-missionary church sins against its own best interest and is inviting defeat. A stay-at-home Christianity is not real Christianity at all.

The hope of the church is missions!

If we are to see a change in this area of worldwide Christian advancement, then the worldwide Church must be awakened to its potential and its destiny. Never before have we had greater opportunities than we currently have in this day and age. The day that the global Church awakens to its Great Commission purpose is the day that Christ's Great Commission mandate will be completed.

Here are three areas that are often listed as the top Three Self-Inflicted Hindrances that have crippled the global Church regarding focusing on and completing the Great Commission:

1. The Issue of Dependency

Dependency occurs when churches or other mission/social programs that are dependent upon foreign funding and/or personnel do not have any strategy or hope to transition the situation to a self-sustaining nationalized work. When conducting mission work and establishing new works abroad we must always, from day one, provide a strategy to make the work self-governing, self-supporting, and self-propagating. This is always better than creating ministry models that the nationals cannot sustain or duplicate.

2. The Misuse of Short-Term Missions Trips

We must make sure that churches do not turn short-term missions trips into a self-serving activity. Over two million people (from the United States alone) take short-term missions trips every year costing over one billion dollars. Regrettably, we are not getting one billion dollars' worth of results. Out of the multitude of short-term missions trips, thirty-three percent of those trips never leave the United States. Please understand, short-term trips are both biblical and needed, but the facts convey that we need to make some major adjustments when it comes to the way we approach short-term missions trips, if we are to see a greater return on the investment of such trips.

The worldwide Church must be awakened to its potential and its destiny.

3. Lack of Genuine Partnership

The body of Christ should not be in competition with each other. It is time that the Church unite for the sake of reaching the world for Christ. Individual churches and pastors should not focus on building their individual kingdoms. If we are going to see the completion of the Great Commission, we must lay aside our own agendas and pick up our Lord's agenda.

The advancement of the Kingdom of God in the world will require genuine partnership with one another. Churches working together. Agencies working with other agencies. Christians working with one another. Each esteeming the other better than themselves. A unity and like-mindedness spoken of in Philippians chapter 2 is what is needed to accomplish the task.

The encouraging news is: **The Great Commission is within our grasp!** Though the Unreached People Groups number in the thousands, the current Church is well able to accomplish the task. There are 1,000 churches for every one Unreached People Group. We have established that fifty-five percent of the world's wealth is in the hands of Christians. There are over 16 million Christian churches in the world today.

The late Dr. Ralph Winter, commenting on the Church rightly stated that, "The Church of the Lord Jesus Christ is **twenty times** stronger than necessary to finish the task, but most of it is dormant."

The completion of the Great Commission is doable! However, it will require an awakening of the Church to a greater level of commitment than we presently have. The Church, once again, must refocus its purpose back on why God created it in the first place. We are not here to simply build ministries. Rather, we as the Church, are here to complete the one mission we were given—that every tribe, tongue, people and nation be reached with the Gospel of our Lord Jesus Christ.

> *The advancement of the Kingdom of God in the world will require genuine partnership with one another.*

GREAT COMMISSION MANDATE
DISCUSSION QUESTIONS:

What did the Great Commandment—Great Commission teaching reveal to you?

How did this session broaden your understanding of the global harvest?

THE GREAT COMMISSION CHURCH

EMPOWER THE PASTOR

*Equipping the pastor to lead the
Church in missions!*

A. The Three Cs

To provide good leadership to any function in the church (including the area of missions) will require what we call The Three Cs:

1. Competency

The pastor must be able to demonstrate a certain level of understanding of missions and be able to gather the necessary people and tools around him/her to build a strong missions church.

2. Confidence

The pastor must have the confidence necessary to lead the church in missions.

- The pastor must be able to build trust in the congregation when it comes to his/her leadership in the area of missions.

- That way, the congregation will buy-in to the church's vision for missions.

3. Commitment

The pastor must communicate and demonstrate that one of the main priorities of the church is missions.

B. Ten Facts Every Pastor Should Know

Fact # 1: *The pastor is the key to a strong missions church.*

The determining factor of whether or not a church will be a missions-minded church is the pastor. We must make no mistake concerning this point. The responsibility falls squarely on the shoulders of the senior pastor. Why? Because the pastor is the visionary leader of the congregation! As the pastor leads, so goes the church. If the pastor isn't excited about missions, doesn't promote missions, and doesn't encourage the people to be involved in missions, the missions program will be seen in the eyes of the people as something that carries little importance concerning the purpose and focus of the church.

This is why the pastor must be empowered to lead the missions charge with passion and confidence.

This passion will become contagious and will eventually stir the hearts of the church's leaders and the whole congregation.

What if the pastor lacks a genuine passion for missions? How can that be changed? Here are three suggestions:

1. **Through Biblical Truth:** The pastor will become passionate for missions through finding out what God says about it. According to Jesus, the whole purpose of the church is to expand the Kingdom of God.

2. **Through Prayer:** Ask God to break our hearts with what breaks His heart, and that is the world! Jesus declared in John 3:16 that God the Father so loved every man, woman and child that He gave His only begotten Son.

3. **Through a Short-Term Missions Trip:** Every congregation should send their pastor on a short-term missions trip.

As the pastor leads, so goes the church.

This provides a first-hand encounter with real missionaries and their missions activities in the field. There is no substitute for this experience. Something special happens in the heart of a Christian while on a missions trip that changes them forever.

Fact # 2: The Church is God's instrument to reach the world.

Before Jesus ascended into heaven in the twenty-eighth chapter of Matthew, He commissioned the Church "to make disciples in all nations." Down through Church history, we have referred to this mandate from Christ as the Great Commission. Missions is a direct response by the Church to carry out that mandate. Missions is not just a program in the Church. It is the purpose of the Church!

God has raised up local congregations to be His instruments to equip the Body, so the Body can carry out His global ministry plan. The local church is the driving and sending force behind every missions endeavor, and is the seedbed for all future missionaries.

Dr. David Shibley, in his book *A Force in the Earth*, makes this bold statement: "Any church that is not vitally involved in missions forfeits its biblical right to exist." These are strong words, but they can also be faith-building words for you as a pastor! Because your church is vitally involved in missions, your church has a God-given right to exist—not only to exist, but also to carry out its destiny in the earth. You are a church of divine purpose with a divine call from Heaven!

Fact # 3: Any size church can have a significant role in missions.

Many churches give up on missions before they ever get started because they think, "What we can do won't matter anyway." Wrong! This is what the devil would want you to

> *The local church is the driving and sending force behind every missions endeavor...*

think. Nothing can be further from the truth. Small churches can do mighty things when it comes to global missions. Your church has been created to be a part of God's worldwide missions movement, and His global plan will suffer if you are not involved to do your part, and the wonderful thing is: You can be!

A few years ago, a pastor contacted Go To Nations by phone and said, "I started a church a few months ago that is not associated with any mainline denomination and currently has thirty-five people in the congregation. My problem is I want my church to be involved in missions, but I don't know how to make missions an important part of the church. Could you help me?"

Immediately, Go To Nations started working with the pastor to initiate the same steps in his church that are included in this *Global Pathway* manual. What a joy it has been to see the progress that church has made with their missions program. The pastor's passion to be a missions church was the real key, and the congregation quickly followed the pastor's example.

But a couple years later, the church faced a major crisis especially for a small congregation. Some churches under the same circumstances may not have survived. But one of the things that kept the people strong and focused as a church was their commitment to missions. The leadership of the church determined that failure was not an option. God was counting on them on a local scale and on a global scale. Too much was at stake for them to give up. That determination has paid off.

Today, that small church is moving forward with God and has a missions budget of $40,000. They actively support a large number of missionaries on a monthly basis. They are involved with several field missions projects and send

Small churches can do mighty things when it comes to global missions.

short-term missions teams from their church on missions trips each year. They accomplished all of this with a congregation of seventy-five members. It is amazing what God can do through small churches when they catch a vision for the world!

In another church of fifty people, the congregation has been actively involved in missions since 1985, mostly through its missions partnership with Go To Nations. The church has given tens of thousands of dollars to missions each year, which has helped impact thousands of people in over ninety nations around the world.

The pastor is quick to admit that being the pastor of the church over the past twenty years has not been an easy task. The church is located in a rural town of 300 people far from any major city. There are no interstate highways close by or large factories or businesses in the area. The countryside is made up mostly of farmland. But still in this remote location, this church has been a beacon of God's love to the small community and a demonstration of how God can use a small church to make a difference on a global scale.

Recently while I was talking to the pastor, he shared something with Go To Nations that I wish every pastor that is serving in a small church could hear. He said, "When you are a pastor of a small church in a small town like I am, every once in a while you would ask yourself: am I really making a difference with my life? Then I think about what our church has been a part of around the world through our missions program. It is at that moment that I have the answer to my own question. Our church is small, but it is a church that is important in God's overall plan. Every time our people hear a missions report of what has been accomplished with our help, it encourages them to do and give their best for the cause of Christ and stay committed to the work of the church."

They accomplished all of this with a congregation of seventy-five members.

Fact # 4: The church's light that shines the farthest shines the brightest at home.

Pastors often ask these questions: "If we really get involved with missions, what effect will it have on my congregation? Will it strengthen it or weaken the overall operations of the church? Will it hurt our finances?" These are very legitimate questions and deserve to be answered.

Through the years, different research studies have shown the more people in a local church that have a heart for missions, the more they have a heart to reach their own community as well. Why? Because a heart for missions is a heart to reach people, help people, and minister to people. When people get excited about reaching the world, it affects the way they act around people in their own neighborhood.

"Missions...will it hurt our finances?"

One thing that most pastors would say concerning their churches is, "We could sure use more resources so we can do more for the Lord." When pastors talk about more resources for their churches, they are generally talking about two things: more people and more money. How would a strong missions program in your church affect those two areas? Let's look at the findings from a research study conducted by the Assemblies of God (AG).

One of the greatest success stories in modern missions has been the foreign missions program of the Assemblies of God. Through their missions programs, millions of people have been reached for Christ around the world with thousands of new churches planted.

From the conception of the Assemblies of God movement, one of their main areas of focus has been world missions. But like every church movement, some of the AG congregations embraced missions more than other AG churches. The church leaders wanted to know what effect this had on both groups of churches. Their research yielded two startling facts:

1. Strong missions churches experienced sixty-seven percent more converts annually than non-missions churches.

2. The people attending strong missions churches received fifteen percent more total per capita income than the members in their non-missions churches.

The conclusion of their study was clear. The AG churches with a strong missions program experienced a significant increase of people and finances over the non-missions AG churches. God loves to bless the work of the local church when that work includes reaching out to the nations of the earth.

A living example of this would be Pastor Dan Betzer, the Pastor of First Assembly of God Church in Fort Myers, Florida. Today, Pastor Betzer is well-respected as a national Christian leader, a successful church builder, and as an anointed teacher of the Word of God.

But when Pastor Betzer started in ministry, he says that things did not go well for him in the beginning. When giving his personal testimony, he often talks about the early years when he was the pastor of a small church that was in financial debt with no natural way to get out of it. In the midst of his desperation, he shares how God gave him a key revelation that he has been building his ministry on since that day.

Pastor Betzer said God told him, "Son, build the church on missions and you will never lack in finances again." But he said, "Lord, the church is in debt with no way to pay the bills. How do I address that?" God replied, "Have a missions convention and raise money for missions. I will take care of the debt." That is exactly what Pastor Betzer did even

God loves to bless the work of the local church when that work includes reaching out to the nations of the earth.

"Son, build the church on missions..."

though it didn't seem logical to raise money for missions when they couldn't even raise money to pay the bills of the church. But the people responded, and their financial situation started changing almost immediately. The offerings got significantly larger, more people started tithing, and the debt of the church started disappearing.

Many years later, Pastor Betzer accepted the Senior Pastor's position at First Assembly of God Church in Fort Myers, Florida. The church had lost a large number of its members resulting in the church getting into deep financial debt. Pastor Betzer knew that he was taking on a real challenge. So, what did Pastor Betzer do to turn the bad situation around? He did exactly what God had told him before. He started building the church on a strong vision for missions.

Today, First Assembly of God Church is a thriving, growing church with new multi-million-dollar facilities. And it is all debt free. Every chance he gets, Pastor Betzer encourages pastors to get vitally involved in missions.

Mike Croslow, a good friend of mine who served as a missionary in Africa for twenty years, shares the story about a meeting he attended with the late Pastor John Osteen, the founder of Lakewood Church in Houston, Texas. Pastor Osteen strongly believed that every church needed a strong missions program. While Pastor Osteen was alive, Lakewood Church gave millions of dollars to missions every year.

Pastor Osteen made this statement: "God has finances reserved for the harvest, and pastors need to learn this! Unless the church gets involved in missions, the congregation will never see that money."

What Pastor Osteen went on to explain was, this is money not taken from the other needs of the church. This is extra money that God wants to supply through the church for the

Every chance he gets, Pastor Betzer encourages pastors to get vitally involved in missions.

purpose of reaching the global harvest. He reemphasized how this brings fresh life to the overall church and new excitement to the congregation.

Fact # 5: *Your church can avoid horror stories concerning missions.*

Many pastors have shied away from missions because of a negative experience they had with a missionary or some missions project. You probably know or have heard of one of these bad situations. We all have! And these experiences have taught us a very important lesson. When missions is not approached in the proper way, it can cause headaches for the pastor, and it can create a mess in the church. But the answer is not to ignore Christ's mandate to the Church and avoid missions; instead, we must allow our past experiences to show us the correct way to do missions.

When we analyze the causes of missions' failures or mishaps that have negatively affected churches over the years, (especially independent churches), the five most common causes are:

1. Most of the churches had no written missions plan that would provide the processes, systems, and guidelines that protect the church from negative experiences.

2. There was no established missions track that provided a foundational process for missionary candidates. For example: if you were a Baptist and wanted to become a missionary, the Baptist denomination had an established track for missionary candidates. If you were a Lutheran, you went down the Lutheran track. If you were a member of the Assemblies of God church, you went down the AG track. If you were a member of an independent church and wanted to become a missionary, most likely, the pastor didn't know what to do with you.

When missions is not approached in the proper way, it can cause headaches for the pastor.

3. There was no process to help someone confirm their call to missions or to evaluate the preparedness and spiritual maturity of those who wanted to be missionaries. This resulted in many going to the mission field with unresolved issues that eventually sabotaged their field ministry.

4. Missionary candidate training was almost nonexistent. In most cases, issues like fund raising, pre-field departure preparation, and field placement procedures had no organized way to be addressed.

5. The church struggled to provide the necessary support services for missionaries once they were on the field. Most of the time, the church did not realize the many needs of the missionary until the missionary was already in the field. This caused major challenges for the church and the missionary.

When it comes to having the church equipped to handle missions in a proper way, one pastor made this statement: "It is a wonder that we had any missionaries who made it. The only ones that did are the ones who simply refused to quit. All we knew to do was pray for them, give them some money, and throw 'em out there to see if they would stick."

Several times a year, Go To Nations conducts a ten-day missionary candidate training program in Jacksonville, Florida. Most of the participants are people who are considering full-time missions service. But another group of people who attend the training regularly are existing field missionaries who want to attend the program as a refresher course. Some veteran missionaries want to attend because they were sent to the field years ago with no initial missionary training. A good example of that would be a precious brother named Jim. He attended our candidate training after serving as a missionary in the Philippines for ten years. On the fifth day of the training in one of the sessions, the instructor noticed

If you ... wanted to become a missionary, most likely, the pastor didn't know what to do with you.

Jim putting his hands over his face and shaking his head from side to side. When the instructor asked Jim if everything was alright, he pulled his hands down from his face and with tears in his eyes he said these words: "Why didn't someone tell me these things ten years ago? It would have saved me so much heartache and grief." The good news is, Jim returned to the mission field after the training program with a new fire and a new sense of confidence and direction.

For a pastor and a church congregation, there is good news: You can do missions right! Do not let some story about a bad missions endeavor stop you from establishing missions in your church.

Your church can have a solid missions program with proven processes that will result in much fruit for the Kingdom, and at the same time, be a blessing to the people and operations of your church. *Global Pathway* will help you take the necessary steps toward seeing that accomplished.

Fact # 6: The landscape of local churches is an ocean of untapped potential.

As we look at the landscape of different church groups across America (USA), it is evident that God is using dedicated people in all of them to reach the harvest. But still a majority of local churches are like virgin soil when it comes to missions mobilization. The potential is almost unlimited. Let me demonstrate what I mean with this example. During the decade of the nineties, the Assemblies of God reached twenty million people for Christ in foreign countries. And this incredible work was accomplished through the missions programs of 12,000 Assemblies of God churches in the United States.

Today, there are over 200,000 independent churches scattered across the United States alone, but ninety percent of these churches do not have an established missions program. Most

Your church can have a solid missions program with proven processes.

of them would say that they are involved in missions. But in reality, it is in a very limited and unorganized way.

Just imagine what could happen if all these churches and others established strong missions programs that maximized their missions effectiveness in the nations. We are talking about hundreds of thousands of churches of untapped potential that God wants unleashed on the world.

Fact # 7: Mega churches will not reach the world for Christ alone.

We live in an age of mass-media presentation that constantly flashes before our eyes the ministries of some of the largest churches and organizations in Church history. But even though we are thankful to God for these wonderful mega ministries that we all admire, and many times, are inspired by what they are accomplishing, don't be fooled into thinking that these great mega ministries are going to reach the world while the smaller ministries sit back and watch. In reality, the mega churches are not going to even lead the charge when it comes to completing the Great Commission.

Why do I say that? Because it is mathematically impossible! Among all the churches today, only two to five percent of them have over a thousand members. The average church size in most countries is under one hundred members.

This means over ninety-five percent of all the churches would be classified as a small church. The group who has to carry the day when it comes to global missions is the little guys, not the mega churches. This is another reason why it is so important for every church to understand its significance when it comes to the global harvest.

Pastor Steve Vickers, president of Harvest Churches International, speaks often about working together with everyone doing their part in world evangelism. Pastor Steve

The group who has to carry the day when it comes to global missions is the little guys.

says, "When that happens, we all accomplish more and pygmies can wave the torches of giants!"

Fact # 8: *Every church has a missionary sitting in the congregation.*

God wants to raise up full-time missionaries from every church congregation. Why? Because the local church is the seedbed for all missionaries! As a church, we are commanded as God's people to take personal ownership of the Great Commission in three distinct ways: We are to pray, we are to go, and we are to send.

Paul Brannan, a true missionary statesman who has dedicated over fifty-five years to global evangelism, once made this statement, "When it comes to the mission field, we have two choices as Christians: We can either go, or send someone else in our place."

But the fact is that most churches have never sent a person from their congregations to the mission field. This is a reality that we must see changed in order for the Body of Christ to reach the world with the Gospel message.

According to the U.S Center for World Mission (Frontier Ventures), there are over 16 million Christian churches in the world and 400,000 missionaries. That is one missionary for every forty churches. If one missionary could be raised up out of every fifteen churches, we could increase our worldwide mission force to over one million.

The reason the Great Commission is not completed is not because it is outside the capability or the grasp of the global Church. It is because we, the Church, haven't truly recognized that we are the generation who can complete the Great Commission.

God wants to raise up full-time missionaries from every church congregation.

For many years, the late Ralph Winter, the founder of the U.S. Center for World Mission (Frontier Ventures), served as a key leader in the effort of awakening the churches to their call to missions and their global potential. From decades of research, he made this declaration: "The Church of the Lord Jesus Christ is twenty times stronger than necessary to finish the task, but most of it is dormant."

Fact # 9: The missions program should be more than the pastor.

A few years ago, Go To Nations was invited to be a part of a leadership conference which was sponsored by a specific network of churches. One of the organized discussion times at the conference was on the subject of the level of missions involvement among their churches. At first glance, their churches seemed to be heavily involved in missions. But after closer examination, that was simply not the case.

Many of the churches in this network had taken on a missions model that is extremely restrictive to the missions activities of the church. The model is: the pastor *is* the missions program! The whole missions program evolves totally around the personal mission outreaches of the pastor while the rest of the church sits dormant in the church pews.

Too many times, pastors travel all over the world exercising his/her ministry gift, while the church congregation at large has no real understanding or opportunity to answer the call to missions on their own lives. No full-time missionaries received any support nor were any missionaries raised up from the congregations.

It is exciting to see pastors personally involved in overseas missions, but that should be a part of the missions program, not the whole thing. Pastors are called to mobilize the whole church to a personal involvement in missions. The pastor's

Pastors are called to mobilize the whole church to a personal involvement in missions.

zeal must be just as great to see that happen as their own personal involvement.

Fact # 10: Missions is a team effort.

It has always been God's plan for missions to be a team effort. There is no place for elitism, territorialism, or individual kingdom building when it comes to the global harvest. God wants the whole Body working together to reach every nation on the face of the earth with the Good News of Jesus Christ. When a church endeavors to carry out their missions program by themselves, the limitations on what they can accomplish will be significantly increased.

With the average church size under one hundred people, most churches do not have the people, the resources, or the missions expertise to make a significant impact in world missions working alone. This is why it is critical for churches to work with other churches and missions agencies in order to maximize everyone's potential in the global harvest.

C. Assess the Current Missions Activities

The first step in moving forward in any area of ministry is to first locate exactly "where you are" in your development. This will give you a clear picture of your current strengths and identify areas for future attention. The Missions Activity Locator is an exercise that will help you in that process.

The main purpose of this tool is to encourage your church by identifying all of its current involvement on missions and to help identify all the untapped potential that lies within it.

Missions Activity Locator–Questionnaire

_____ 1. Does the church's leadership see missions as one of the high priorities of the church?

_____ 2. Have any full-time cross-cultural missionaries been raised up from within the congregation?

_____ 3. Is the congregation being taught about the scriptural basis for missions?

_____ 4. Do you pray as a congregation for the nations and for the missionaries?

_____ 5. Are testimonies or reports about missions given in the church service at least on a quarterly basis?

_____ 6. Does the church support any field missions projects?

_____ 7. Does the church have an annual missions conference?

_____ 8. Does the church receive faith promises from the congregation for the missions program?

_____ 9. Do 50% or more of the families in the congregation participate personally in missions giving?

_____ 10. Is 10% of the general budget designated for foreign missions?

_____ 11. Does the church have a Missions Sunday each month?

_____ 12. Are missions emphasized by the pastor from the pulpit?

_____ 13. Are missions highlighted by an attractive, well-placed bulletin board or table that is frequently updated?

_____ 14. Is active missions participation encouraged by and within all departments in the church?
(Example: Youth, Children, Singles, etc.)

_____ 15. Does the church have a written missions plan stating its vision for missions, including policies, procedures, and budget process?

_____ 16. Does the church have a Missions Director?

_____ 17. Does the church have a Missions Advancement Team (missions committee)?

_____ 18. Has the church's leadership attended any missions training programs?

_____ 19. Do you have a process for people in your congregation who want to pursue full-time missions service?

_____ 20. Does the church have at least two missionary speakers each year?

_____ 21. Does the church take the initiative to find out if the missionaries have any special needs?

_____ 22. Does the church have any established process to help take care of missionaries when they come home to visit?

_____ 23. Has the pastor been on a short-term missions trip in the past two years?

_____ 24. Is there at least one short-term missions trip taken by the congregation per year?

_____ 25. Does the youth group take an annual short-term missions trip overseas?

_____ **Total number of "yes" answers**

Missions Activity Locator Chart

23–25	First-Class Missions Church
19–22	Strong Great Commission Church
10–18	A Church on the Move
5–9	Great Opportunity for Increase
0–4	Ready to get Started

Note: Go To Nations is prepared to help your church address any of the issues covered in the questionnaire. How can we help you?

EMPOWER THE PASTOR
DISCUSSION QUESTION:

Which of the "Ten Facts" were the most thought provoking to you?

ENVISION THE CORE

There is always a special group of people in every church that the pastor greatly depends on to help him promote buy-in and move forward with the congregation concerning the direction of the church. This group is what I am calling the Core.

Envisioning the Core is a strategic process that will prepare the congregation to embrace wholeheartedly the church's mission program.

The Core Gathering

The Core is usually made up of three distinct groups. The first group is the church's leadership, such as the children's pastor, youth pastor, associate pastors, church administrator, and so on. The second group is made up of the influencers of the church. Every church has a few key couples that carry tremendous influence with the congregation, but they are not official leadership. The third group of people is those who have demonstrated a personal burden or passion for missions. You may have four or five people that you feel would fall into this third category. Besides the excitement they will bring to the Core, the importance of this group will be explained in greater detail later in this section.

Before unleashing a whole new level of missions activities on the church, it is important for you as the pastor to gather the Core together in an informal, intimate setting. If a church has one hundred members, the Core gathering may be around twenty members. Meeting in someone's home sometimes adds a special touch to the gathering, or you can meet at the church if that is more convenient.

At this setting, you take the opportunity, as the pastor, to open your heart and share your passion and commitment to missions. But it is also important that the Core understands that your commitment to missions is not just a personal preference, but it is God's scriptural destiny for the Church.

In order for the church's leaders and the congregation, as a whole, to truly embrace the vision for missions of the church, they need to know two important things:

1. Missions is a biblical mandate from God. The church's congregation needs to be shown scripturally that God has called them to play a critical role in missions—individually and corporately as a church.

2. God has given instruction on how the Church can effectively carry out its vision for missions. In other words, the church's congregation needs to understand that the pastor knows how to lead the church forward in the area of missions.

When the congregation has the awareness and assurance that God is calling the local church to a greater role in missions, their buy-in will be no problem. The five points described in the following sections marked A–E will serve as foundational keys to help you "Envision the Core." Sections A and B deal with the scriptural side of missions. Sections C, D, and E deal with the practical application of how the missions program of the church will be carried out.

It is critical that the pastor start systematically sharing these five envisioning keys from the pulpit to the whole congregation soon after the Core gathering has taken place.

A. Great Commission Call

The first genuine step to envisioning people for missions is to lead them to the revelation that missions isn't some activity that Christians decide whether or not they want to be involved in. Missions is God's mandate to every born-again believer. The moment a person accepts Jesus Christ as

Missions isn't some activity that Christians decide whether or not they want to be involved in.

their Lord and Savior, God calls them into the ministry of reconciling this world back to its Creator (2 Corinthians 5:18).

A common word used in missions circles is the word *personalization*. It means to "take ownership of something, to accept something as your responsibility." This is exactly what God wants us to do, as Christians, concerning the Great Commission. He wants us to take ownership of the Great Commission. In other words, it is our *calling*, not a good activity to consider. God wants us to make the Great Commission our personal commission!

A few years ago, I was ministering in a small home group on God's plan for world evangelism. After sharing a few simple truths from the Bible, one of the ladies of the group could no longer contain herself. She bellowed out with a loud voice, "My Lord, we are all called to missions!" Through a few simple verses, God opened her eyes to the awesome global call that is on every Christian.

In Matthew 28:19, Jesus gives us this command, "Go therefore and make disciples of all nations..." This is our commission as believers!

Even though we looked at Matthew 28:19, the Great Commission was given by Jesus in some form in all four Gospels and in the Book of Acts. (Mark 16:15-18; Luke 24:46-48; John 20:21; Acts 1:8)

Too many times Christians read these verses and relate them to a small group of specialized cross-cultural missionaries. But in reality, these verses are to identify the awesome global call on every believer. In other words, Jesus wants the whole congregation to be a part of taking the whole Gospel to the whole world!

Once while I was visiting a church in the United States, a member of the congregation approached me and made

God wants us to make the Great Commission our personal commission!

Envision the Core

this statement, "I understand how important you are in the Kingdom of God." "What do you mean?" I asked. He said, "Because you are a missionary, the call of God on your life to reach all those nations is a large and important one." I appreciated the respect he had for me as a missionary, but with all sincerity I looked straight into the face of the man and said, "My friend, don't underestimate the call of God on your own life. God is counting on you to use your life to help reach the nations. It may be in a different role from mine, but He is counting on you to be a part of completing the Great Commission just as much as me."

The biggest misunderstanding in the Body of Christ today concerning missions that we must correct is—Missions is not a special call to a chosen few. Missions is the mandate of Christ to every Christian.

B. Great Commission Church

Understanding the corporate calling on the local church to missions is vital when envisioning the Core. While Jesus was on the earth, He set three key events in motion:

1. Jesus birthed the Church. (John 20:22)
2. Jesus commissioned the Church. (Mark 16:15)
3. Jesus empowered the Church to carry out the Commission. (Acts 1:8)

God has established the local church as His instrument in the earth to unify the efforts of individuals for the sake of the global harvest. The local church is the sending force behind every missions endeavor and the seedbed for all future missionaries.

In Matthew 24:14, Jesus declares, "And this gospel of the kingdom shall be preached in the whole world for a witness unto all nations, and then shall the end come." The larger the percentage of the congregation that is personally involved in missions, the sooner the Body of Christ will complete the Great Commission. History will be delayed until the Church completes its mandate.

An important element of a strong Great Commission church is a clear understanding of Acts 1:8, because Jesus instructs us to reach our community and reach the nations of the world at the same time. He said, "But YOU will receive power when the Holy Spirit comes on YOU; and YOU will be my witnesses in Jerusalem, <u>and</u> in all Judea <u>and</u> Samaria, <u>and</u> to the ends of the earth."

Today, there are some churches that have no intention to be involved with missions. They are not involved in reaching the nations for Christ in any way. When asked why, these churches would say that God has called them to reach their neighborhood and surrounding communities. They consider their neighborhoods as the extent of their mission field! And they believe this is scriptural.

These churches are right, but only half right. It is God's mandate for every church to reach out to their own community (or we could say, their own Jerusalem). But that is only a portion of Acts 1:8. Every Christian individually and every church corporately has a local call and a global call at the same time. It is not an either/or situation. It is both.

While speaking to a pastor one day about developing a missions program in his church, he told me, "My church is not ready for a missions program." I asked him, "What do you mean?" He said, "We haven't reached our own city yet with the gospel. And Jesus instructed us to reach our Jerusalem, and then, the other parts of the world."

I understood the thinking behind the pastor's statement, but as we examine Acts 1:8 a little closer, we find that the pastor's interpretation of the verse was incorrect. Jesus never used the word "then." He was very clear in saying, "...Jerusalem

History will be delayed until the Church completes its mandate.

Envision the Core

and in all Judea *and* Samaria *and* to the ends of the earth." If Jesus expected us to stay home and not evangelize outside our home town until it was totally reached with the Gospel, then every missions trip that the Apostle Paul took would have been unscriptural! God is no respecter of persons; God wants the Church to carry out its local call and its global call simultaneously.

If Jesus has made the completion of the Great Commission the calling of each Christian and the corporate calling of every local church, how is that calling going to be fulfilled? The answer is through a team effort.

In Romans 10:14–15 (KJV), the Bible gives us a divine plan by which this team effort is to take place. The Apostle Paul lays out a strategy by asking these questions: "How then shall they call on Him in whom they have not believed? And how shall they believe in Him of whom they have not heard? And how shall they hear without a preacher? And how shall they preach unless they are sent?"

From these two verses, we can identify two distinct and equally important roles of the local church concerning God's missions plan. The first distinct role refers to those who are identified as "sent ones." One of Paul's questions (paraphrased) is simply this: How can the congregation help reach the nations without identifying someone to go and then having the church send them?

It is from verses like Romans 10:15 that the Church has adapted the term "missionary." The word comes from the Latin word *missio*, which means "sent one." Through history, it has been used to refer to people who were sent by the Church to minister cross-culturally. So, by following the words of the Apostle Paul for global evangelism, the Church is to identify, equip and send missionaries from the congregation to foreign lands. These missionaries are scripturally known as "sent ones."

God wants the Church to carry out its local call and its global call simultaneously.

Missionaries are scripturally known as "sent ones."

The second distinct role we see in God's team effort from the Book of Romans is the role of "senders." This is the role of every member of the local congregation, and is equally as important as the role of a sent one. Without senders, you do not have sent ones! This identifies the local church as the sending force behind every missionary and missions endeavors.

But you may ask, is there an example in Scripture where the early Church actually carried out Romans 10:14–15? The answer is yes! In Acts 13:1–3, we find these words:

> Now there were in the church that was at Antioch certain prophets and teachers; as Barnabas, and Simeon that was called Niger, and Lucius of Cyrene, and Manaen, which had been brought up with Herod the tetrarch, and Saul. As they ministered to the Lord, and fasted, the Holy Ghost said, Separate me Barnabas and Saul for the work whereunto I have called them. And when they had fasted and prayed, and laid their hands on them, they *sent them away*. (KJV)

The church at Antioch was carrying out exactly what the Apostle Paul taught us in Romans 10. A congregation of believers had been established in the city of Antioch in which Paul was a part. After a time of prayer and fasting, Paul and Barnabas were identified to the leadership by the Holy Spirit that they were to be the "sent ones" from the church body. In other words, the Holy Spirit was commanding the church to give up Paul and Barnabas for the missions work that they were called to fulfill. So, the church leaders obeyed the Lord and gave up some of their best members and diverted some of their resources to be used in another work that was outside the needs of their own church.

Regardless of how useful Paul and Barnabas were to the church at Antioch, the brethren faithfully obeyed. With

Without senders, you do not have sent ones.

a true spirit of faith, they gave up their self-interests, and with prayer, fasting, and aid, they *sent* them forth. Paul and Barnabas were the "sent ones," and the rest of the congregation served the missions cause as "senders." This began the first recorded missionary journey of Paul and Barnabas from their "home" church in Antioch to neighboring provinces surrounding the Mediterranean Sea.

The congregation at Antioch—through their fellowship with the missionaries, their obedience to Christ's Great Commission mandate, and submitting to the leading of the Holy Spirit—was instrumental in many souls being saved. While they certainly would have been able to accomplish many things in the city of Antioch with these men, there was an additional principle at work of stretching beyond themselves to reach others in distant lands.

C. Missions—Not Just Another Program

To carry out any type of missions activity in the church will require a certain amount of organization. This constitutes having an established missions program with some staffing positions, whether they are filled with full-time or volunteer personnel. But it is important that the missions program isn't viewed or treated like any other department of ministry in the church, because there is one major difference between the missions department and every other department.

The missions department should be like a thread that runs through every part of the church. For example, missions should be a part of the new believers training program. Missions should be an important part of what we are teaching and exposing to our children and youth.

A good example of this would be something that took place in one of my supporting churches. The children always requested to be in the main service when I was ministering

Paul and Barnabas were the "sent ones," and the rest of the congregation served the missions cause as "senders."

at the church rather than in the separate Children's Church service. Here is the reason why:

The Children's Pastor taught the children about missions on a regular basis. She would read Scriptures dealing with reaching the lost, and then they prayed for the different nations of the world and for the missionaries that the church supported. They learned they could be a vital part of the missions program of the church even as little children. Each child had a picture of me, and the Children's Pastor always read my newsletters out loud. Then the children discussed what they heard. These children were pumped with excitement when it came to missions!

So, when I came to town, the children could hardly wait. They sat in the front row because they wanted to see in person their missionary whom they had prayed for and heard so much about.

The last time I was at the church on a Sunday morning, I brought with me a big framed world map. I had all the children come forward and lay their little hands on the different nations and pray. They ran forward and crowded around the map and prayed with all their hearts. It was a powerful time, and it had a profound effect on the rest of the congregation.

Missions should serve as a unifying force that brings every department of the church together for a common purpose.

When my grandmother was eighty-five years old, she would meet at the church with her Senior Citizen's group three days a week at 7:00 a.m. One day I asked her, "Grandma, I know it is a lot of effort for you to meet with the rest of those elderly ladies early in the morning and so often. Why do you do it?" She looked at me with a big smile and said, "Yes, it is a little hard to get this old body going some mornings, but us ladies enjoy being together, and we feel like we are doing something with our lives that counts for something.

Missions should serve as a unifying force that brings every department of the church together for a common purpose.

Envision the Core

You see—we gather together at the church and make quilts, beautiful bed quilts. When we finish one, we sell it and give the money to the missions fund. It's a way I can make a difference even at my age."

D. Four Main Areas of Activation

In order to establish a strong missions program in the church, the Core must understand that the church must be prepared to address these four areas:

Envisioning:

You must instill a vision in the congregation for the global harvest by imparting an understanding of missions from God's perspective. Missions is not a concept or idea that some denomination came up with. God is the one who instituted missions.

As long as missions is only seen by the congregation as something the pastor is excited about, their zeal to embrace the church's vision for missions will be minimal. But when the people see missions as a part of their God-given calling and destiny, they will take personal ownership of it.

Dr. George Murray, the founder and President of Columbia International University and Seminary once said, "We should be as evangelistic with believers about missions as we are evangelistic to the lost about salvation."

Mobilizing:

You must mobilize the people into a personal involvement in missions. This breaks down into three main missions activities: Going, Sending, and Praying.

Missions is not a concept or idea that some denomination came up with.

...three main missions activities: Going, Sending, and Praying.

In the context of the local church, Dr. Larry Reesor, the founder of Global Focus, describes mobilization in this way: "Mobilization is teaching believers to understand God's global plan, motivating them to a loving response to God's Word, and providing opportunities for them to use their gifts, abilities, and resources individually and corporately to accomplish His global plan."

Training:

You must provide the necessary training to equip the congregation with the understanding about missions and the tools to be effective in missions. Training processes must be established to prepare people for short-term and full-time cross-cultural missions service.

A key to a long, fruitful ministry is proper preparation and training on the front end. Excellent missions training programs are available to the local church to help you equip your people.

A key to a long, fruitful ministry is proper preparation and training on the front end.

Serving:

Every missions endeavor requires a certain amount of supply services to help sustain the longevity of the program. A strong missions program is never maintained by the efforts of the pastor alone. God wants to raise up missions leadership that will help the pastor run with the vision for missions. (The next section will deal with this more.) Also supplying support services to full-time missionaries would fall under this category. This is where missions agencies can offer some real assistance and expertise.

E. Missions Advancement Team

To carry out any type of missions activity in the church will require a certain amount of organization and manpower.

One of the reasons pastors sometimes shy away from establishing a strong missions program is that they are afraid that it will consume their time and energy, which are already in short supply. To help you develop and carry forward the missions plan of the church, I suggest that you create a Missions Advancement Team (MAT) that is led by a Missions Director. In the formative stages, the pastor usually serves in the director's role until one can be appointed. The purpose of the MAT is to provide a leadership forum (or committee) for the activities regarding missions and to assist the Missions Director and Senior Pastor in carrying out the vision for missions of the church. The goal of the MAT is to facilitate the development and involvement of the congregation into a world-class missions church.

This is where the "Envision the Core" gathering comes into play. It is important for them to understand the need and the overall function of the Missions Advancement Team. But not only that, from the people attending the gathering you want to recruit those who will help you form the MAT. Hopefully, from the Core you will find your initial members. This is why one of the groups we identified to invite to the gathering were people from the congregation that have demonstrated in the past a personal burden or interest in missions. These people will bring a genuine excitement and passion to the team.

You also want to recruit people who will supply the leadership and organizational skills needed for the MAT to function effectively.

Concerning the Missions Advancement Team, there are two main areas that you need to explain at the Core gathering:

1. The formation process.
2. The primary responsibilities.

Create a Missions Advancement Team (MAT) that is led by a Missions Director.

By giving some explanation to these two areas, the Core will understand the main functions of the MAT and understand how you need to move forward in the process. Here is a simple outline that can be used to share with the Core:

Formation Process:

1. Initiated by the pastor.
2. Usually made up of volunteer members with the exception of the Missions Director in some cases.
3. Serves the pastor as a working committee.

Primary Responsibilities:

1. Create and maintain a Written Missions Plan.
2. Find ways to create Missions Awareness among the congregation.
3. Develop a Missions Prayer Initiative in the church.
4. Organize and conduct an Annual Missions Conference.
5. Schedule and Implement Short-Term Missions Trips.
6. Establish a process for raising up Full-time Missionaries.
7. Create and maintain an Annual Missions Calendar.

It is important that you do not allow the list of responsibilities to intimidate the Core. More than anything, this list should be presented from a visionary perspective to help show the incredible potential that lies before the church concerning missions. There are materials available for every one of these responsibilities that will equip the Missions Advancement Team in the developmental and implementation processes.

One of the main goals of the "Envision the Core" gathering is to identify people you would like to appoint to the Missions Advancement Team. It is up to your discretion how you carry out this process. You may want to ask the

...show the incredible potential that lies before the church concerning missions.

group to prayerfully consider serving on the MAT, and you will follow up by contacting them individually. Or you may want to hand pick the initial team and not give an open invitation. I recommend five to seven members.

The main thing is that you move forward and not allow a long-time lapse in forming the MAT. Once the vision has been cast, you want to maintain the momentum you have created.

Envision the Core
Discussion Questions:

In this session, what spoke to you the most?

Do you think most Christians understand they are personally called to missions?

If not, why not?

ESTABLISH A PLAN

*Establishing a plan enables your congregation
to rally around a clarified strategy that will help
your church maximize its potential in the global harvest.*

A. Activate the Missions Advancement Team

Until the Missions Advancement Team is activated, all the work of taking the missions program forward will fall on the shoulders of the pastor. This is why it is critical to have a functioning Missions Advancement Team as soon as possible.

Most pastors do not have the time or the energy that developing the missions program will require. The MAT will supply you with the manpower needed to develop and implement the missions plan. This allows you, as the pastor, to function more in a visionary, oversight role rather than in the developmental, operational, and maintenance aspects.

B. Write the Missions Plan

The first task of the Missions Advancement Team is to write the draft for the Missions Plan. The oversight and final approval of this process will require the pastor's involvement. The Missions Plan will establish many of the guidelines by which the MAT will function.

Habakkuk 2:2 teaches us a powerful principle with these words: "And the Lord answered me and said, 'Write the vision, and make it plain upon tables, that he may run that readeth it.'" The investment of putting your vision for missions on paper will pay great dividends for the Kingdom of God and for the overall well-being of your church. It will enable your congregation to rally around a clarified strategic plan that will help your church maximize its involvement in the global harvest. The process will require prayer, accumulated input from the church's leadership, and several team work sessions. But the eternal results that you experience from it will make it worth all the effort.

Why Create a Missions Plan?

1. To ensure that the missions outreach of the local congregation is given top priority in prayer, financial support and involvement in every area of the church as you attempt to obey the Great Commission.

2. To assist in providing a coordinated missions effort that will be mutually beneficial to both the local church as well as to missions.

3. To develop and maintain a clear vision of purpose and a harmony of effort in all activities that relate to missions in the local congregation.

4. To help make wise decisions that affect missions in a manner that is consistent and systematic in nature.

5. To avoid making important decisions solely on the basis of emotion.

6. To ensure that missions funds are administered both effectively and faithfully.

7. To inform and equip members of the church to be actively involved in missions on a personal level.

8. To maintain the highest level of accountability in every aspect of missions.

Your vision for missions on paper will pay great dividends for the Kingdom of God.

How Do We Get Started?

In most tasks, getting started is half the battle. Many churches never get started in developing any type of missions plan because the task seems too intimidating. What should the missions program include and address? What format should I use in order to develop a missions program that will be useful and productive? Who should be involved in the process?

The information in this section is designed to help you address these questions. It will present a systematic format that will enable your church to clarify its missions plan with a new sense of direction and purpose. The following pages serve as a prototype or sample of a written missions plan from which you can glean ideas and information.

It is important to realize that the written plan presented is to function as an example only. You should take each section and customize it to make it express your particular heart, vision, and church's structure. Some parts you may use word for word. Other parts you may change entirely.

The Missions Plan sample is not meant to be an all-inclusive template covering every missions situation imaginable. It is designed to be a good foundational model for any size congregation that wants to be an effective missions church. For this reason, you may need to add special sections to your missions plan dealing with a specific issue in your church that is not covered in this sample.

In most small churches, the pastor may serve as the interim Missions Director and lead in the establishing of the MAT until other people can be identified and trained to step in.

Once a written missions plan is developed by the MAT, the Missions Director submits it to the Senior Pastor or

Getting started is half the battle.

You may need to add special sections to your missions plan.

Elder Board. The developmental and approval process may be adjusted to fit the particular leadership structure of your church.

Note: The Practical Guide: A Blueprint for writing your missions plan is included directly after the Discussion Questions for this section.

C. Develop Operational Procedures

Usually the written Missions Plan is not meant to be an all-inclusive manual that covers every step-by-step process for every missions activity of the church. Other supplemental manuals are normally used to accomplish that goal.

Operational procedures and job descriptions for the different missions activities will not be completed before you launch your missions program. Developing the step-by-step processes for your missions functions is an on-going task. Here is a list of areas for which you will eventually need to establish operational procedures:

1. Missions Director and Advancement Team
2. Annual Missions Planning and Budget Process
3. Annual Missions Conference
4. Short-Term Missions Trips
5. Missionary Candidates
6. Missions Prayer Initiative
7. Track for Full-Time Missionary Service

D. Annual Missions Calendar

If it doesn't get scheduled, it doesn't happen!

A simple principle to remember is: If it doesn't get scheduled, it doesn't happen! This is especially true in the context of the local church. Most churches have a master calendar on which every department's schedule of events are overlaid in such a manner that it all works together.

In order to include the missions activities into the church's master calendar, the Missions Advancement Team needs to plan out all the known missions activities and events for the coming year into an annual missions calendar. Here is a list of things to consider:

1. Annual Missions Conference
2. Missions Sundays
3. Missionary speakers
4. Missions Advancement Team meetings
5. Short-term missions trips
6. Missions prayer events
7. Missions seminars and workshops

Establish a Plan
Discussion Questions:

Why is a written missions plan important?

How does this plan help/benefit the pastor and the church?

A Blueprint
For Writing Your Missions Plan

A Practical Guide
To Help Churches Make Their Vision for Missions
Come Alive

A Prototype

A BLUEPRINT...FOR WRITING YOUR MISSIONS PLAN

Table of Contents

Formative:

1. **Missions Director** 91
   - A. Purpose
   - B. Term of Office
   - C. Qualifications
   - D. Duties

2. **Creating a Missions Advancement Team** 93
   - A. Purpose
   - B. Structure
   - C. Meeting Frequency
   - D. Term of Service
   - E. Qualifications

3. **Primary Focus of the Missions Advancement Team** 95
   - A. Envisioning
   - B. Mobilizing
   - C. Training
   - D. Serving

4. **Responsibilities of the Missions Advancement Team** 97
   - A. Primary Responsibilities
   - B. Functional Responsibilities

Operational:

5. General 99
   A. Definition of Missions
   B. Scriptural Basis
   C. Purpose
   D. Flexibility of Interpretation

6. Financial Policies 101
   A. Preparation and Approval of the Annual Missions Budget
   B. Raising Up Missions Funds
   C. Allocation of Missions Funds
   D. Funds Shortage Policy
   E. Funds Surplus Policy
   F. Allocation of Missions Administration Cost in the Church
   G. Support Level of Missionaries
   H. When Missionary Support Begins
   I. When Missionary Support Ends
   J. Honorarium for Visiting Missionary Speakers
   K. Support of Missionary Families
   L. Insurance for Missionaries
   M. Education of Missionary Children
   N. Missionary Retirement
   O. Evaluation and Revision of Support
   P. Scholarships for Missionary Candidates

7. Policies for Full-Time Missionary Service 105
   A. Philosophy
   B. Procedure for Selecting New Candidates to Support
   C. Missionaries from other Churches Soliciting Support
   D. Nature of Work of Missionaries Accepted
   E. Missionary Support during Educational Leave
   F. Guidelines for Missionary Furloughs

8. The Use of Missions Agencies 109
   A. Philosophy of the Church

B. Responsibilities of the Sending Church
C. Responsibilities of the Missionary
D. Responsibilities of the Missions Agency
E. Supporting Churches

1

Missions Director

A. Purpose

The Missions Director serves as the head of the Missions Advancement Team and provides organization and coordination for the overall missions plans of the church.

B. Term of Office

The Missions Director is appointed by the Senior Pastor and will serve until excused from the position by the Senior Pastor. The Missions Director can be a church staff position or volunteer based on the needs and abilities of the church.

C. Qualifications

1. Possesses a strong passion for global evangelization.
2. Has competent leadership skills.
3. Knows how to administrate projects.
4. Has a good working relationship with the Senior Pastor.
5. Is actively involved in missions through prayer and giving.
6. Has been on a short-term missions trip or has served as a cross-cultural missionary.

Prototype

Missions Director

D. Duties

The Missions Director shall be responsible to:

1. Serve as the head of the Missions Advancement Team.
2. Submit an annual Missions Plan with budget.
3. Lead the Missions Advancement Team in accomplishing all their assigned duties.
4. Stay abreast with the world missions movement.
5. Establish any offices or committees needed on the Missions Advancement Team.
6. Lead in an annual evaluation of the progress of the church's vision based on the missions plans.

2

Creating a Missions Advancement Team (MAT)

A. Purpose

1. To provide a leadership forum for the missions activities of the church.
2. To assist the Missions Director and the Senior Pastor in fulfilling the vision for missions of the church.
3. To facilitate the development of the church as a world class missions church.

B. Structure

1. The MAT is directed by the Missions Director.
2. The Missions Director is appointed by and reports to the Senior Pastor.
3. The Senior Pastor may attend any MAT meeting at his/her discretion.
4. The MAT will consist of four to five members and one director.

C. Meeting Frequency

1. The MAT will meet on a monthly basis.
2. Meetings will be scheduled by the Missions Director.
3. One meeting annually should be devoted to the review of missions policies and procedures.
4. The Missions Director may call special meetings as needed.

Prototype

Creating a Missions Advancement Team (MAT)

D. Term of Service

1. The initial members of the MAT will be appointed by the Senior Pastor.
2. The Missions Director and the Senior Pastor will submit nominations for appointment of additional members of the MAT.
3. Members will serve a three-year term with a second optional term by approval of the MAT.
4. The term of the Missions Director shall be indefinite or until determined by the Senior Pastor.

E. Qualifications

1. An active member in good standing of the church.
2. In agreement with the Statement of Faith of the church.
3. Committed to prayer for the leadership of the church and the nations of the world.
4. Demonstrates an active involvement in the church's missions program.
5. Tithes and is a committed financial supporter and advocate of world missions.
6. Able to invest the time required for effective participation and not be overcommitted with other church activities.

3

Primary Focus of the Missions Advancement Team

One of the overall functions of the MAT is to develop an on-going strategy to address these four areas:

A. Envisioning

Help the pastor instill a vision for the global harvest in every segment of the church body.

1. Every member understands that they are called to missions.
2. Every member takes personal ownership of the Great Commission.

B. Mobilizing

Assist the pastor in mobilizing people into a personal involvement in missions.

1. Recruitment of missionary candidates.
2. Short-term missions opportunities.
3. Missions giving.
4. Organized Prayer Initiative for Missions.

C. Training

Provide people with the necessary training and preparation tools that equip them for effective cross-cultural missions ministry.

Primary Focus of the Missions Advancement Team

1. Candidate track for full-time missionary service.
2. Specialized in-church missions training workshops/seminars.

D. Serving

Supply support services for full-time missionaries, church missions projects and in-church missions activities.

1. Missions Advancement Team activities.
2. Special church missions events.
3. Special volunteers/helpers.

Note: For further explanation, see Chapter 4-A.

4

Responsibilities of the Missions Advancement Team

A. Primary Responsibilities

1. Write the Missions Plan.
2. Annual Missions Calendar.
3. Annual Missions Conference.
4. Short-Term Missions Trips Schedule.
5. Process for Full-Time Missionary Service.
6. Strategy of activities for Envisioning, Mobilizing, Training, and Serving.
7. Missions Prayer Initiative.

B. Functional Responsibilities

1. Attend scheduled MAT meetings.
2. Ensure that the missionary effort of the church remains focused on the Great Commission ministry.
3. Develop and maintain a written missions plan with an annual review.
4. Bring missions awareness to the congregation.
5. Assist in administering the various missions components of the church.
6. Establish a missions prayer initiative and be actively involved.
7. Assist in the planning and implementation of an annual missions conference and other special missions events.
8. Establish a process for missionary service for potential candidates from the congregation.

Responsibilities of the MISSIONS ADVANCEMENT TEAM

9. Recommend funds allocation concerning the church's missions giving.
10. Review requests from missionaries seeking financial support and relationship with the church.
11. Assist the Missions Director in communicating with missionaries sent or supported by the church.
12. Facilitate the care of missionaries while they are in town.
13. Assist in recruiting, evaluating, and selecting candidates for missionary service.
14. Serve as a liaison between the church, missionaries, sending agencies, and other organizations.
15. Create and manage an annual missions calendar.
16. Assist the Missions Director in preparing an annual missions budget to be submitted to the Senior Pastor (See Appendix A).
17. Assist the Missions Director in establishing one-year, two-year, and three-year missions goals to be submitted to the Senior Pastor.
18. Serve as a liaison between the congregation, missionaries, and agencies.

5

General

A. Definition of Missions

Missions is any endeavor aimed toward the goal of reaching beyond the needs of the local congregation for the purpose of fulfilling the Great Commission by proclaiming the gospel of Jesus Christ, making disciples, and relating to spiritual and physical needs of mankind, including mercy ministry, relief, and development. The policies and procedures of this manual relate to cross-cultural overseas ministry and some cross-cultural exceptions within the borders of your own country. Missions is not to be confused with benevolence within the community of the church. Those needs will be addressed through other church policies and activities.

B. Scriptural Basis

The missions efforts of our church are based on the eternal truth of God's Word as revealed in Genesis 12:1–3; Matthew 22:3; Matthew 24:14; Acts 1:8; Romans 10:14–15; Romans 15:20, and Revelation 5:9.

C. Purpose

The purpose of _____ Missions program is to faithfully respond to Christ's Great Commission mandate and to maximize the involvement in the global harvest as a congregation. The following policies and procedures have been established to accomplish the following:

1. Achieve a clear sense of direction in carrying out the church's vision for missions.
2. Avoid making important decisions on an emotional or haphazard basis.

General

3. Ensure that each dollar given to missions is spent as God would have it spent.
4. Maintain consistency and clarity of strategy as the Missions Advancement Team members change.
5. Develop Christ-like accountability throughout the entire church's missions program.

D. Flexibility of Interpretation

These missions policies, which are updated periodically by the Missions Advancement Team and approved by the Senior Pastor, are to be used as a guideline for all major missions decisions. The policies cover approximately ninety percent of all questions or problems that may arise regarding the missions program in the church. For those items not covered or when exceptions to the policy are deemed necessary, a proposal is drawn up by the Missions Advancement Team through a majority consensus and submitted to the Senior Pastor for approval. The missions plan with its policies shall be reviewed and revised annually by the Missions Advancement Team and submitted to the Senior Pastor for approval.

6

Financial Policies

A. Preparation and Approval of the Annual Missions Budget

The Missions Director shall be responsible for presenting an annual Missions Budget to the Senior Pastor for approval. The Missions Advancement Team is responsible for writing the budget based on projected needs and goals. This process should start in September each year and be presented to the Senior Pastor by the first of December for the ensuing year.

B. Raising up Missions Funds

Finances for the church's missions budget shall be raised by using three primary methods:

1. First, 10% of the collection of tithes and offerings of the congregation are allocated toward the missions program.
2. Second, finances will be raised for the missions budget through a Faith Promise Giving Campaign during the annual missions conference of the church.
3. Third, finances will be raised for missions through special missions fund-raising projects.

C. Allocation of Missions Funds

The overall strategy for allocation of missions funds breaks down as follows:

1. 50% shall be used for the support of full-time missionaries.
2. 10% shall be used for the support of national workers.
3. 10% shall be used for the support of missions agencies or for missions support ministries.
4. 10% shall be used for short-term missions trips/missions scholarships.

Financial Policies

5. 5% shall be used for cross-cultural home missions.
6. 5% shall be used for the annual missions conference.
7. 10% set aside in a contingency fund.

After proper research and evaluation, the MAT shall submit recommendations for the allocation of missions funds to the Senior Pastor for approval.

D. Funds Shortage Policy

If, after undertaking the missions budget and a Faith Promise program, the expected monies are not received, the church shall then do the following:

1. Communicate this need to the congregation and ask them to earnestly pray about the situation.
2. The Elder Board shall meet to see if money can be taken from the general budget to offset the difference.
3. If needed, the church shall have a fund-raising event for this cause.

E. Funds Surplus Policy

All of the surplus missions funds are considered discretionary funds. These funds shall be kept in a contingency fund or emergency funds designated for unforeseen circumstances, both tragic and joyous, concerning the missionaries or missions-related activities. The MAT may submit recommendations to the Senior Pastor for the allocation of these funds. The funds may be reserved for the budget of the coming missions year if not used.

F. Allocation of Missions Administration Cost in the Church

Normally, the church shall not have missions administration costs because all the work shall be done by the regular church staff or under the direction of the MAT on a volunteer basis. However, if a unique unexpected need arises, this money shall be taken out of discretionary funds with the approval of the Senior Pastor.

G. Support Level for Missionaries

The starting monthly support levels for full-time missionaries will be:
- Singles— $100
- Couples—$200

Monthly missionary support shall increase at a rate of $50 per year of service if additional funds are available. Maximum support for missionaries from the church is $500 and $300 for missionaries from other churches. Additional funds may be allotted for ministry projects on a one-time basis or on a monthly basis.

H. When Missionary Support Begins

Normally, the support shall begin in January each year. This is when the church's annual budget goes into effect. Support for a missionary may start anytime during the year if recommended by the MAT and approved by the Senior Pastor.

I. When Missionary Support Ends

Regular monthly support will be carried over each year if the missionary complies with all reporting requirements and is in good standing with the Missions Director. If a missionary desires to end his/her missionary service, the church will continue the support for three months after the missionary returns to his/her home country. This only applies if the missionary leaves missionary service in good standing and has served on the mission field for a minimum of four years.

J. Honorarium for Visiting Missionary Speakers

On the day that the visiting missionary speaks, a special offering shall be received to offset his/her expenses.

K. Support of Missionary Families

The church shall start at the same amount of support to each missionary regardless the size of his/her family. However, special consideration shall be given if there is a husband/wife team on the mission field that are both conducting considerable ministry activity. The church shall consider this as being two missionaries and the support shall then be doubled.

Financial Policies

L. Insurance for Missionaries

The church shall not be responsible for the insurance of the missionaries we support. The provision of insurance shall be the responsibility of the missionary.

M. Education of Missionary Children

The church shall not be responsible for including in the annual budget any amount for the educational financial support of the children of the missionaries. However, missionaries may submit special requests for funds to the MAT for review.

N. Missionary Retirement

The church shall not be responsible for including in the annual budget any amount for the retirement of the missionary. A retirement plan is the responsibility of the missionary.

O. Evaluation and Revision of Support

Each year the annual church's budget is reviewed and recommended for the next calendar year. All increases in the missionaries' support will be determined by this budget review.

P. Scholarships for Missionary Candidates

The church shall offer limited scholarships for those who demonstrate a genuine call to the mission field and are pursuing missionary candidate preparation and training.

7

Policies for Full-Time Missionary Service

A. Philosophy

History has demonstrated that full-time missionaries can impact entire nations. Traditionally, missionaries would spend a lifetime in a single country and only infrequently return to their country of origin. Today missionaries characteristically serve shorter terms than in the past, but full-time missionaries are still the backbone for reaching the world for Christ and discipling those who are evangelized. Media, literature, and other influences are positive, but it is the full-time missionary who is on the ground, part of the community, and willing to commit for the long haul that gives the long-term results that change nations. A large percentage of our missions funds will be dedicated to the support of this cause.

B. Procedure for Selecting New Candidates to Support

Anyone desiring to be sent out from the church and receive financial support as a full-time missionary must be approved by following the procedures established in the ***Steps to the Mission Field*** manual.

C. Missionaries from Other Churches Soliciting Support

Our church recognizes the need for the Body of Christ to work together when it comes to supporting missionaries. Few churches have the capability to underwrite the total amount of missions support that a missionary needs to live in a foreign country and conduct missions ministry. The average missionary has to build a support team consisting of churches, friends, and relatives who will financially partner with the missionary in order to reach one hundred percent of their missionary budget. For this reason, the church accepts requests for missionary support from people outside the membership of our church. The following steps are required by the missionary:

1. Complete the application for missionary support using the forms provided and mail to the Missions Director with a recommendation from your pastor and two personal recommendations using the forms provided.
2. Set an appointment to meet with the Missions Director of the church.
3. If the proper criteria have been reviewed and met, an interview with the MAT will be scheduled.
4. The MAT will submit their recommendation to the Senior Pastor for approval through the Missions Director.

The areas of responsibility for the Missions Director before and during the personal interview with the missionary:

1. Review the application and recommendations.
2. Discuss any of the submitted information as deemed necessary.
3. Schedule an interview with the MAT if the missionary meets eligibility.

D. Nature of Work for Missionaries Accepted

As in a local church setting, missions work requires a variety of ministry gifts to be successful. These giftings may enroll the missionary into ministry responsibilities that are foundational to missions works such as evangelism, church planting, leadership, community transformation or relief work, and discipleship. Other missionaries may serve in a more supportive role such as administration, helps, bookkeeping, and hospitality. Each missionary requesting missionary support will be evaluated on an individual basis, based on the needs of the field location and the effectiveness of their ministry on world evangelism.

E. Missionary Support during Educational Leave

Missionaries pursuing further education that will strengthen their missions service shall continue to receive support for one year if approved by the Missions Director. The leave will only be considered after four years of missions service on the field.

F. Guidelines for Missionary Furloughs

We recognize the need for a missionary to be given time for rest, family, and itineration. However, to maintain a level of effectiveness in the field, the missionary is expected to spend no more than two months per year in their home country. After four years of missions service on the field, a longer furlough should be considered. This is a general guideline that may need adjustment based on individual situations. Missionaries serving through missions agencies will receive the expertise of the agency in dealing with this area.

8

The Use of Missions Agencies

A. Philosophy of the Church

In order to conduct missions ministry with a high level of integrity and excellence, and to help us maximize our potential in the global harvest, the church often works with missions agencies as a partner in missions endeavors. Missions agencies serve as a support ministry in helping us carry out the vision for missions. They provide certain tools and areas of expertise in the area of cross-cultural missions ministry that are not generally found in the context of the local church.

Sending out a missionary through a missions agency for missions service creates an important three-way relationship between the sending church, the agency, and the missionary. Each one of these parties embraces certain responsibilities in order to maximize the strength and fruitfulness of the relationship.

B. Responsibilities of the Sending Church

The sending church will:

1. Establish a relationship wherein it has the opportunity to assess and confirm a person's/family's gifts and the call to missionary service.
2. Work closely with the missionary candidate and the missions agency to ensure that the standards set forth by the church are met.

Prototype

The Use of Missions Agencies

3. Insist that the missionary candidate understands the inner workings of the church and its requirements for missionary service.
4. Formally commission the missionary before the church congregation.
5. Take on a percentage for the support of the missionary candidate commensurate with the church's membership and financial resources.
6. Make it possible for the pastor (and/or members) to visit missionaries where they serve in order to minister to the missionaries and increase the scope of the pastor's vision for missions.
7. Educate the congregation to their missions responsibility.
8. Maintain close communication with the missionaries so that the congregation may pray more effectively for the needs of the missionary.
9. Be ready and willing to work with the missions agency and the missionary if a significant problem arises on the field.
10. Be actively involved with debriefing the missionary and on-going accountability during their home assignment.
11. Communicate with missionaries about church news and prayer needs.
12. Encourage the missionary in ministry and personal growth.
13. Involve the missions agency when there is a major decision to be made regarding the missionary's ministry, relocation, or well-being.
14. Uphold the missions agency's reporting requirements of missionary funding and projects according to the ministry standards of the Evangelical Council of Financial Accountability (ECFA) in the U.S. or similar accountability organization in your country.
15. Supply the leadership of the church with updated reports on the status of the missionaries and projects.
16. Impart apostolic oversight. (The sending church is not necessarily the congregation that gives the missionary the most money, where he/she spent the most time growing up, where the extended family attends, or even where he/she first felt called to missionary service. All or many of these may be true, but they are not prerequisites of a sending church.)
17. Take the primary responsibility of partnership with the missions agency in the care and supervision of the missionary.

C. Responsibilities of the Missionary

The Missionary will:

1. Have full recommendation for missionary service from the church and the missions agency.
2. Have a clear sense of calling (both husband and wife, if applicable) from God for missionary service.
3. Meet all the preparation requirements for missionary service, whether required by the church or the missions agency through which the missionary will be serving.
4. Identify the expectations of the church and/or missions agency regarding the prospective service and whether the missionary is willing to meet these expectations to the best of his/her ability.
5. Accept the responsibility of on-going accountability to the sending church and the field leadership of the missions agency.
6. Report regularly to the sending church on their personal well-being, ministry effectiveness, and annual ministry goals.
7. Develop and maintain a strong financial and prayer support base with interested churches and individuals based on required support levels set by the church or the missions agency.
8. Consult with the sending church and the field leadership of the missions agency regarding any major change in assignment or location.
9. Be responsible to comply with the Internal Revenue Service (IRS) regulations in the U.S. or the corresponding agency in your country.
10. Set aside, when on home assignment, significant time for face-to-face contact with the leadership of the church, length of time and frequency to be agreed upon in advance.
11. View the relationship between the church and the missions agency (if used) as sacred and such a relationship will not create an adversarial environment in order to serve his/her own purposes.
12. Demonstrate a spirit of teamwork by cooperating and contributing toward the common good of the team and the project in the field.
13. Function according to the missions policies of the church and the missions agency.
14. Comply with the laws of the land unless they are in direct violation of Scripture.
15. Attend a local church on the mission field and participate in its programs when it is possible, to avoid the habit of going to church only when you minister, in order to stay spiritually healthy.

The Use of Missions Agencies

D. Responsibilities of the Missions Agency

The missions agency will:

1. Recognize the church as the sending body and serve as a partner in the process.
2. Seek to understand the overall vision for missions of the missionary and plans of the sending church in order to facilitate them as much as possible.
3. Serve as a catalyst in closing the communication loop between the missionary and the church.
4. Provide training and a mobilization track clearly identifying the missionary candidate's future steps and procedures for missions service.
5. Ensure there is an enthusiastic recommendation for all missionary candidates by the sending church which affirms the candidate's Christian maturity, missionary call, gifting, and experience.
6. Work closely with the missionary candidate to help them through the itineration process.
7. Require the missionary candidate to remain in their home country and not depart to their field assignment until he/she has completed or meets all the criteria established by the sending church and the missions agency.
8. Provide field oversight via supervisory structures on the field and/or from the Headquarters of the missions agency.
9. Consult with the sending church on any major changes concerning the missionary's ministry focus, relocation, or personal well-being. The missions agency will work with the missionary to ensure that all supporting churches are advised of important changes in a timely manner.
10. Make available the missions agency's field leadership and the Headquarters leadership for the purpose of consultation and problem solving to the sending church and its missionary candidates.
11. Upon request, supply the sending church with a copy of the missions agency's reports and financial statements.

E. Supporting Churches

Besides the three primary parties previously listed, a fourth party also plays an important role. The fourth party is the other churches that are supporting the missionary. In most cases the church does not have any jurisdiction over these supporting churches; however, from a philosophical standpoint, here are the responsibilities we believe the supporting church should embrace, and we should embrace, as a supporting church to other missionaries.

Supporting churches will:

1. Give toward the financial support of the missionary's personal and ministry budgets.
2. Have the right to require unreserved commendation from the missionary's sending church.
3. Have the right to be informed of major decisions affecting the missionary's ministry and location and ask for accountability from the missionary and the missions agency.
4. Be asked to provide home assignment help, various types of missionary care, etc.
5. Be given information, upon request, concerning the ministry, well-being and progress of a missionary from the sending church and the missions agency.
6. Have limited involvement in the decision-making process.

LAUNCH THE CONGREGATION

6

By empowering the pastor, envisioning the Core, and establishing a plan, you have laid the foundation to launch the whole congregation into an active involvement in missions.

A. Activate Every Part of the Church

It is important to revisit the section titled "Four Main Areas of Activation" that you shared with the Core gathering. The section deals with the dynamics of envisioning, mobilizing, training, and serving. These four areas give the Missions Advancement Team a working outline for developing a strategy for launching the congregation into missions ministry. I recommend that the MAT take one area of activation at a time and apply it to each function of the church.

For example, let's start developing a strategy to launch the Children's Church in the missions plan:

Area of Activation	Children's Church
Envision	Teach Bible lessons on missions. Tell missionary stories. Study the world map. Show pictures of Unreached People Groups.
Mobilize	Pray for the nations. Take missions offerings. Pray for the missionaries. Write letters of encouragement to the missionaries.

Launch the Congregation 115

Train	Have missionary guests speak to the children. Teach them about giving to missions Teach them the "Senders—Sent Ones" principle. Have foreign guests speak about their country.
Serve	Participate in the annual missions conference. Conduct missions skits and songs in church services. Make gifts and cards for the missionaries. Participate in missions fund-raising events.

Each department of the church can become as creative as they want in developing a strategy for these four areas. Again, the key is to apply all four areas of activation to every part of the church.

B. Annual Missions Conference

Why it is important?

One of the most effective ways to launch the congregation into missions is through an annual missions conference. It will be hard to create or maintain any strong missions momentum without it.

At the same time, it is important to understand that having a missions conference is not an effective way to initiate the development of a missions program for the church. Several key components should be in place first so the church can capture and maximize what God accomplishes in the missions conference.

The key is to apply all four areas of activation to every part of the church.

In Section 7, we will examine a Quick Reference Sheet that addresses eleven action steps. You will notice at that time that "Conduct an Annual Missions Conference" is Step #10 out of the series. Once the church has implemented the first nine steps, they will be positioned to carry out the missions conference in strength and with great effectiveness.

There are three common types of missions conferences when it comes to their primary purpose:

1. To minister to the overall well-being of the missionaries.

    This is when a church encourages their missionaries to come off the field so the church can minister to them. This ministering can be done through building them up through preaching and teaching of the word of God, through special times of recreation and fun, and by providing some practical services. Such services include personal counseling, financial expertise, medical care, shopping sprees, and hair and body care, and so on. All of this can be organized around a weekend of activities and special church services. In other words, the goal of the conference, with all its extra activities, is to minister to the missionaries—spirit, soul, and body.

2. To activate the congregation into a personal involvement in missions.

    The main purpose for this kind of missions conference is to envision and activate every church member into a personal involvement with the church's vision for missions.

3. A combination of the first two types.

The annual missions conference that is presented in the pages ahead deals with the second one. This type of missions conference will allow you to achieve the following:

One of the most effective ways to launch the congregation into missions is through an annual missions conference.

- Initiate a missions-giving strategy.
- Involve the entire congregation (adults, teens, and children).
- Present the missions call to everybody, "a call to all."
- Increase consistent personal giving.
- Strengthen the entire missions budget.

The annual missions conference should be seen by the congregation as the "Super Bowl" event among the yearly activities of the church, and one of the primary responsibilities of the Missions Advancement Team. Much time, energy, and careful planning will be required to conduct a fruitful missions conference.

Note: See Appendix C for a Missions Conference Planner Worksheet

How will it benefit the church?

When a local church gets involved with reaching the lost nations of the world—which is the heart of God—it will create many positive results for the church. Here are eight ways your church will be blessed:

1. **A missions conference is the most effective way to open the world to your congregation.** The average person does not naturally contemplate the spiritual condition of the world from any real sense of understanding. By providing an understanding of the dire spiritual need of the world, your people will be better equipped to pray, give, and go.

2. **A missions conference will make your people more soul conscious.** The Assemblies of God report that AG churches that conduct an annual missions conference have sixty-seven percent more converts per year

than AG churches that do not conduct any missions conference.

3. **A missions conference turns the focus of your church OUTWARD.** A church that has an inward focus is a church filled with challenges and criticism. Churches with a strong emphasis on missions tend to have people with more joy. Joyful Christians get along better with each other and make better workers.

4. **A missions conference helps unify the church.** Your congregation is unified around a common goal that will have a positive effect on every area of the church.

5. **A missions conference will generate more money for missions.** When incorporating the Faith Promise Giving service in the missions conference, most churches more than double their missions giving in the first year.

6. **A missions conference provides your congregation opportunity.** The Bible commands every Christian to play a vital role in the Great Commission mandate. The missions conference activates your people to pray, to give, and to go to the mission field.

7. **A missions conference brings financial blessing to the lives of your people.** Studies have shown that offerings to the general fund of the church usually increase because God blesses the people for their giving to missions. This results in bigger tithes and offerings in the weekly offertory.

8. **A missions conference helps the local church fulfill its God-given purpose.** The local church is God's instrument in the earth for world evangelism. The local church is the seedbed for all missionaries, and is the sending force behind all missionaries.

Launch the Congregation

What should be accomplished?

In order to maximize the potential of an annual missions conference, here is what you want to see happen:

- The missions conference should be eye-opening. By sharing the spiritual need of the world, the congregation will be educated to the global task that is before God's Church.

- The missions conference should be heart-moving. A dull, dry missions message that comes simply from the standpoint of duty will not be successful. Our emotions must be touched before we will respond willingly and enthusiastically. Every service should move the hearts of the people.

- The missions conference should initiate action. The purpose of the conference is to bring each person in the congregation to a point of a personal involvement in the church's missions program. Every Christian should embrace the Great Commission by either going to the nations as a full-time missionary or help send others through their prayers and financial support. A missions conference provides the means for that to happen.

Main highlight of the missions conference:

The highlight of every conference should be the Faith Promise Service. If this is a new concept to your church, you may need to educate your people to the potential and benefits of Faith Promise Giving. This can be accomplished slowly during your preaching times leading up to the week of the conference. Faith promises should be received in the service with the largest attendance, usually the Sunday morning worship service. Everyone, including the occasional attendee and the uncommitted, should have an opportunity to obey the Great Commission through giving. Not all people will

Every service should move the hearts of the people.

Everyone should have an opportunity to obey the Great Commission through giving.

totally grasp the Faith Promise concept immediately, but many will make a nominal monthly commitment, and that is a beginning.

What is a Faith Promise?

The Faith Promise service is based on 2 Corinthians 8:3 where the Apostle Paul wrote to the church at Corinth about the giving of the Macedonian Christians. Paul said:

> For I testify that according <u>to their ability</u>, and <u>beyond their ability</u>, they gave of their own accord...

As Christians, we can respond financially to the Great Commission in the same way the Macedonians did. First, we can give according to our ability. This means to give out of our "known resources." In other words, we should make giving to missions a part of our monthly budget, the resources we know we have. Every Christian has a certain level of income. God wants us to make reaching the world a priority when it comes to the way we use that income.

For example, the average amount families spend on cable or satellite TV could range from $25 to $150 a month or more. Shouldn't we give as much to help reach lost and hurting people with the Good News of Jesus Christ as we spend on TV? This is what is meant by budgeted giving or giving according to *our ability*.

Second, Faith Promise Giving brings us into a whole new level of giving because it rests confidently in God's ability to provide, not solely on a believer's ability to pay. We, as Christians, can use our faith to tap into God's resources for the global harvest. As matter of fact, that is exactly what God wants us to do. This is what the Macedonian Christians did! They used their faith to be able to give *beyond their ability*. A Faith Promise is a spiritual agreement between the Christian and God that, with His help, he or she will give

> *As Christians, we can respond financially to the Great Commission in the same way the Macedonians did.*

a predetermined amount to the church to be used in world missions as the Lord provides.

Why should Faith Promise Giving be implemented?

- Its methods are tried and proven by thousands of churches.
- It creates a personal involvement concerning the Great Commission.
- It will result in increased missions giving.
- In most cases, general fund giving will increase.
- God's blessings will rest upon the local congregation.
- It ties the church member closer to the vision of the church.

Important Questions to Consider:

Here are some common questions that need to be addressed when preparing for a missions conference:

- **How long should a missions conference last?**

    This will be determined by the personality of your church as much as anything. In years past, it was common for churches to have conferences that lasted several days. But in recent times, most churches find it difficult to schedule a multi-day conference due to the busy lifestyle of most Christians. The complex schedules that most modern families keep have cut deep into their ability to attend multiple church services in the same week.

    For this reason, most churches schedule a weekend missions conference based largely on what their people are used to. Here are some variations to consider:

    Saturday Evening: Missions Dinner Banquet
    Sunday Morning: Faith Promise Service
    Sunday Evening: Call to Serve Service

...as Christians, we can use our faith to tap into God's resources for the global harvest.

Schedule your mission conference based on what works in your church.

Saturday Evening:	Missions Dinner Banquet
Sunday Morning:	Faith Promise Service
Sunday Morning:	Faith Promise Service
Sunday Evening:	Call to Serve Service
Sunday Morning:	Faith Promise Service
Missions Banquet	Immediately Following Service

- **How often should we have a missions conference?**

For maximum results, it is critical that you have a missions conference every year. Paul Brannan, a national leader in promoting global evangelism, is a strong advocate of the annual missions conference. Paul exhorts pastors everywhere to "get started and don't stop." Paul states that one of the biggest mistakes that pastors make in maintaining strong missions programs is with their lack of consistency in conducting an annual missions conference. He has noticed that if a church stays consistent for three years in a row in having the conference, the missions program becomes strong and vibrant.

Some churches have a mini missions conference at the six-month mark because of rapid growth of the church and to help heighten the missions awareness in the congregation. But with the effective use of the scheduled monthly Missions Sunday and having a missionary speak in the church on a quarterly basis, a second missions conference in the same year isn't necessary for most churches.

- **When is the best time of the year?**

The best time to schedule a missions conference is not the same for every church. Here are eight things to consider:

"Get started and don't stop."

Launch the Congregation

1. What time of the year does your church have the highest attendance?
2. Is weather a factor in your area of the country?
3. Do not schedule the missions conference when another in-church activity is going on in the same week.
4. Stay away from national holidays.
5. Check to see if there are any community events scheduled in which your congregation may be involved.
6. Stay away from major school events like sports finals week or graduations.
7. Set the date and start planning your missions conference at least six months in advance.
8. Plan your conference for the same month each year. This creates consistency.

- **How do we build excitement for the missions conference?**

Excitement for the missions conference is built by creating anticipation. Start promoting the conference at least four weeks in advance.

Every Sunday during those four weeks do something special to create interest in missions. This can be accomplished through dramas, video reports from missionaries, or a number of other ways. Special news clips demonstrating the spiritual condition of a certain area or country can help bring awareness for the need of global missions outreach.

- **How much money should be spent on a missions conference?**

This will be determined by the financial capability of your church and how much importance you place on the missions program. Anything that is done with excellence will require some finances. Conducting a missions conference is no different. But it is worth the investment!

Do not schedule the missions conference when another in-church activity is going on in the same week.

Build momentum toward the date of your missions conference.

In order to take the planning process forward, it is important that a missions conference budget be established.

Note: See Appendix D for a Missions Conference Budget Worksheet

- **Who should be the speaker(s)?**

Having the right speaker for each service is crucial to the success of the missions conference. For the Faith Promise service to be the highlight of the conference, the speaker for this service should be able to accomplish the following:

1. Be a motivating and interesting speaker.
2. Present a world view of missions rather than focusing on a particular field.
3. Help educate your people to their personal responsibility in carrying out global missions.
4. Be capable of presenting the Faith Promise plan and inspiring your people to action.
5. Must clearly understand the purpose and goals of the missions conference and be willing to work toward them.

- **Should we use missionaries for missions conference speakers?**

Missionaries can be excellent conference speakers or terrible conference speakers based on the criteria we have already established. Even though most missionaries are dedicated workers in the harvest, not all missionaries have the gift of public speaking. The strengths of having a missionary for your conference speaker are their passion for missions and their first-hand experience with cross-cultural ministry in a foreign country. Their weaknesses may be their overemphasis on their missions

Missions conferences are worth the investment.

project with an inability to stay focused on the purpose and the goals of the conference. And most missionaries are not familiar with how to conduct a Faith Promise service, so close evaluation is needed before making a decision.

Close evaluation is needed before choosing a missions conference speaker.

- **How many speakers are needed?**

Many times, this is determined by two factors: the size of the conference budget and the length of the conference pertaining to the number of services. If the missions conference is a weekend event with only two scheduled services, one speaker usually speaks in both services. But it is really up to the discretion of the pastor on how many speakers are used.

- **Who should coordinate the development of the missions conference?**

The planning and the coordinating of the missions conference should be handled by the Missions Advancement Team. This is one of their primary responsibilities, and it keeps the weight of the conference off the pastor. Give your Missions Advancement Team members the opportunity to dream and create.

Keep the weight of the conference off the pastor.

- **Who in the church should get involved?**

The more people you can get involved, the greater success the missions conference will be. If people are involved with the preparation and activities of the missions conference, they will take on a sense of ownership rather than act like a passive bystander. The Missions Advancement Team should actively find ways for church members to be involved. Here are some ways to include different members of your church:

Decoration: Use people to help create a visual world missions theme by hanging flags of the different nations, pictures of foreign lands and different ethnic peoples, any needed props for dramas, etc.

Parades: Have children, teens and adults dress in native costumes and parade in front of the congregation representing the nations of the world.

Skits: Use the youth to put on short, promotional skits during the Sunday morning service the second and third weeks before the missions conference to help prepare the people.

Banquet: All ages can be involved in cooking special dishes from other lands and in the decoration of the tables and the fellowship hall.

Booths and displays: Missionaries, children, youth, and adults can display field projects or different needs (spiritual and physical) that are in the different nations.

Worship Team: Prepare a special worship service with songs about reaching the nations.

Prayer: Special prayer should be coordinated to undergird the missions conference. People who cannot be involved in other ways can serve in this important area.

- **How do we prepare the congregation concerning Faith Promise Giving?**

The week before the missions conference, the senior pastor should preach on missions in the Sunday morning service. The purpose for this is to show the people that the pastor believes in missions and wants to see missions established as a high priority of the church. At this time, the pastor should introduce Faith Promise Giving to the

Find ways for church members to be involved.

The Senior Pastor sets the tone for the missions conference.

congregation and state the church's goal. A brochure explaining the Faith Promise principle should be handed out to everyone in the congregation.

It is never acceptable for the pastor to be gone or to be absent during the missions conference even if other speakers are arranged. The absence of the pastor sends the message to the congregation that missions is not important enough to require his/her presence.

- **Is it important to set a financial goal for the Faith Promise Giving service?**

Yes! By setting a goal, you help the congregation to understand exactly what amount the church is believing God for. It also encourages them to play a significant role in reaching that goal.

To help you determine what the goal should be, keep these things in mind: First, seek God for direction. Sometimes, God will give you a specific figure. Others times, God will have you determine what you think the faith level of the congregation should be. Second, the goal should always be higher than last year's goal, and it should always be at a level that will require faith. Third, even though your goal should require faith, don't set an unrealistic goal in relation to the size of your church. It is always better to exceed your goal than to fall extremely short.

To help you determine what is possible, identify the number of families you have in your church. Then determine what you think the average giving level per family would be. Take the estimated giving level times the number of families in the church. Once you come up with a figure, pray about how much you should add to it for the supernatural move of God.

The Faith Promise Giving goal for the missions conference should be announced to the congregation by the pastor the week before the missions conference. The people should be encouraged to pray about what they think God wants them to do personally.

- **What printed materials will we need?**

The two most common printing needs are a brochure explaining the Faith Promise Giving principle and the Faith Promise card. You may want a banner or banners printed expressing your missions theme. (See Appendix E for the Faith Promise Brochure text. See Appendix F for the Faith Promise Card text.)

Order of the Faith Promise Service:

The Faith Promise service has many of the same components as a regular Sunday morning service, but there should be some extra components to help make the service special and different from a normal Sunday. It is recommended that you keep the service the same length of time as normal. If it runs long, some of the congregation may have to leave before the Faith Promise offering/giving.

Here are some things to consider when putting together your schedule of service:

Worship: Your worship time should be different and fresh from the usual routine. The worship songs should be upbeat, motivating and focused on the nations. This is a time of celebration and declaration. If you are having a parade of nations, incorporate it into the worship service. Use video images, dancers, drama, and so on to help the worship time be special.

Plan out your Faith Promise service.

Launch the Congregation

Offertory: Receive your tithes and offerings as usual, but instruct the congregation that this isn't the Faith Promise offering/giving or missions offering. That will come later.

Announcements: Make the announcements as brief as possible. Handle as much of them as possible through the bulletin or video monitors using short clips.

Communion: This can be a delicate issue in some churches, especially churches that celebrate communion every service. In those cases, you would definitely include communion in the service schedule. You may want to consider having communion at a different point in the service in order to maintain a good flow in the service with the Faith Promise appeal. If your church is not accustomed to having communion every service, I recommend that you do not have communion for the sake of time. Of course, all of this is subject to the leading of the Holy Spirit.

Avoid unnecessary activities during the missions conference.

Special Activities: Do not schedule special activities during the missions conference like Sunday School attendance awards, baby dedications, water baptisms, and so on. These things could divert the attention away from your focus on missions and cause a problem with the time.

Speaker's time: The normal length of church services varies greatly between churches. If Faith Promise Giving is new to the congregation, it is important that the speaker clearly explains the Faith Promise principle, and then effectively shows the congregation how they can respond. In order to accomplish this, the speaker may use a video or a PowerPoint presentation combined with a short message that leads up to the Faith Promise appeal. If the congregation is accustomed to a forty-five-minute message, allow one hour (as possible) for the speaker. If the speaker's time needs to be shorter, it is important that the speaker understands how much time he/she has.

Faith Promise Appeal: Remember—the Faith Promise appeal will take more time than a regular offering. Here are the reasons why:

1. The ushers will have Faith Promise response cards to pass out to the congregation at the signal of the speaker.
2. The speaker will have to explain how to use the response card.
3. The speaker will pray asking for the Holy Spirit to lead the people in their giving.
4. The people will fill out the card.
5. Once the card is filled out, the people raise the card in the air for an usher to collect it.
6. Optional: If you want to collect the cards and add up the amounts committed during the service; you must allow time for that also. It can be exciting for the congregation to know immediately how much was given, and it can lead into a short time of celebration to close out the service.

The Importance of Prayer:

Prayer is the foundation of every Christian endeavor. Mobilizing a team of people to pray for the missions conference is essential. Here are some areas the team can lift up in prayer:

- Pray for the pastor and the leadership of the church.
- Pray for the Missions Advancement Team as they lead in the preparation for the missions conference.
- Pray for the order of service.
- Pray that God would prepare the hearts of the congregation.
- Pray for good attendance.
- Pray for the speaker(s).
- Pray that all the audio/visual equipment will work properly.

Allow adequate time for the Faith Promise appeal.

Launch the Congregation

- Pray for the worship team and all the participants of any special drama, parades, or music.
- Pray for an increase of the vision for missions in the whole congregation.
- Pray that the church will meet the financial goal.
- Pray for the missionaries and projects that the church presently supports.
- Pray that God will call forth new missionaries from the congregation.

Follow-up to the Missions Conference:

Like any major event in your church, quality time should be devoted to a debriefing process where you evaluate every segment of the missions conference. You can determine who should be involved in the process. An evaluation sheet could be distributed to all who were involved, and then have the Missions Advancement Team review all the sheets from which a summary could be prepared. Here are some areas to look at:

Attendance: Was your attendance up or down from what you anticipated? In either case, try to identify the causing factors. Strengthen the positive factors and eliminate the negative factors.

Financial response: Check the Faith Promises received and estimate the amount of solid income for the next year designated for missions. This will help you with your missions planning and help you set a missions budget for the coming year. Remember to set money aside for next year's missions conference.

Date: Determine if the date worked well for the church's schedule and the congregation's schedule. Set the dates for next year's conference, and get them recorded on the master calendar of the church.

Devote time to a debriefing process after the missions conference.

Preparation: The strength or weakness of an event starts with the preparation process. Determine how well or how poorly you did in these areas:

- Did you have time to plan and prepare for the conference?
- Were there certain needed components of the conference missing?
- Was the event too busy, not allowing ample time for what was important?
- Were the people prepared for the Faith Promise service?
- Were the participants properly prepared and knew what to do?

Speaker(s): Since the speakers are such a major part of the missions conference service, it is essential that you evaluate if you are getting the right kind of speakers. Here are some things to consider:

- Was the speaker informative, inspirational, and motivational?
- Did the speaker stay within the goals of the missions conference?
- Did the speaker do a good job explaining and initiating the Faith Promise Giving?
- Did the congregation connect with the speaker?

The calendars of good, anointed ministers can fill up quickly. Book your speaker(s) for next year as soon as possible.

Coordination: Determine how well the Missions Advancement Team handled overall coordination of the missions conference.

- Was the event well organized?
- Were the right people in charge?
- Did the Missions Advancement Team effectively recruit the right members from the congregation and utilize their gifts and talents?

Determine what you did well and what areas you can improve for next year's conference.

Worship: In many ways, the worship team sets the tone for the whole service and should help tie all the segments of the service together.

- Was the right music chosen?
- Did the worship team do anything out of the ordinary to make the conference service special?
- Was the worship used effectively to enhance the other parts of the service?

Decorations: Symbolism is a powerful tool to help the people maintain focus and to set the right atmosphere for a missions conference. The right decorations can make that happen.

- Did the church auditorium look special?
- Did the surroundings speak of the nations, the global needs, and the world harvest?

Missions Sunday: In order to maintain the momentum created by the annual missions conference, it is essential to schedule a monthly Missions Sunday. This should be coordinated by the Missions Advancement Team with the approval of the pastor.

C. Maintaining your Missions Momentum

It is not enough to have a successful Faith Promise response from the congregation at the missions conference. It is just as important to keep the missions interest of the whole church high throughout the year. The challenge of missions must be kept fresh in the minds of the people. Here are some ways to accomplish that:

- **The Pastor:** If the pastor forgets about missions after the conference and never talks about missions or never preaches about the global harvest, the congregation will quickly forget about missions also. The people

The challenge of missions must be kept fresh in the minds of the people.

need to hear the pastor's passion for lost souls and for the church's involvement in reaching the nations on a consistent basis.

- **Missionary Speakers:** Schedule a missionary speaker in the church at least three times a year. This will assure that everyone attending your church will receive regular exposure to missions besides the annual missions conference. If you have multi-services on Sunday morning, use the missionary speaker in all of them. Give the people the opportunity to respond financially to the missionary's need when possible.

  On some occasions you may choose not to give the missionary the full ministry time, especially if the missionary's gifting is not preaching. In those cases, an effective approach could be to conduct an interview with the missionary by asking him/her questions about their missions work. Make sure the missionary is briefed with the questions ahead of time and is prepared to give an informative and exciting response.

  Another way to use your missionary speakers is to have them give a five-minute testimony to the congregation. They should state: Who they are, What they do, and Where and Why the church should be involved.

- **Missions Bulletin Board:** To help keep your people informed about the different missions activities and missionaries that the church supports, create an attractive missions bulletin board. Use the Missions Advancement Team to create it and to maintain it with interesting and current missions facts, news, and special prayer requests. The missions bulletin board is also a great way to display the church's current missions giving compared to the church's Faith Promise total for the year.

Keep missions in front of the congregation.

Launch the Congregation

Be creative in developing the layout for your bulletin board. You may want to have a monthly featured missionary family. Highlight interesting facts about certain countries where your missionaries work. The main thing is that it catches the attention of people when they walk through the church and reminds them of the importance of the church's missions program. The best location for the bulletin board is in a well-trafficked area with good lighting.

- **Prayer for the Harvest:** Form missions prayer groups for these purposes:

  1. Pray for the ministries and needs of the missionaries.
  2. Pray for the spiritual climate of the countries where your church supports missions works.
  3. Pray for more people to become missionaries according to Luke 10:2.
  4. Pray for more people to go on short-term missions trips.
  5. Pray for the leaders of nations that they turn to God.

Cover your missions endeavors with prayer.

A great systematic prayer tool for the global harvest is *Operation World* by Jason Mandryk.

- **Short-term Missions Trips:** By taking teams of people from your church on short-term missions trips, you will light a fire in them for souls and for global missions that will pay big dividends for your church for years to come. There is something about a missions trip that is hard to explain. People are never the same again. A whole new world is opened up to them that causes them to be more thankful and more responsible toward God with their time, talents, and resources.

The excitement and passion that a missions team brings back to the church from a short-term trip will transfer to the people in your congregation. That excitement is contagious! The whole church will become more passionate about reaching their community as well as the world. It will help missions giving stay strong because the people will understand its importance in a whole new way.

- **Missions Materials:** If you have a bookstore in your church, display missions brochures, books, and materials that will stimulate and educate your people concerning missions.

D. Monthly Missions Sunday

Having a planned Missions Sunday each month is a key component in maintaining the momentum that you created through the annual missions conference. The primary cause of decreased Faith Promise giving through the year is a failure to keep missions in front of the people in a fresh and exciting way. How well you implement Missions Sunday is a major factor in determining how strong your missions program and funding will be.

You do not have to devote the whole service to missions on Missions Sunday, but you do need to devote enough time in the service to accomplish two things: First, the people are inspired and motivated to stay faithful to the funding of the church's missions program. Second, take a special missions offering separate from the regular offertory. This will offer the people an opportunity to give their monthly Faith Promise commitment. Some churches place a special container at the front of the congregation, and ask the people to bring their missions offering forward and place it in the container personally. This usually takes place right after the regular offering to help minimize the amount of time needed for the two offerings.

The excitement generated by a short-term missions trip is contagious.

Be creative with your monthly Missions Sunday.

Use different ways each Missions Sunday to help bring missions awareness to and participation from the congregation. Here are a few suggestions to consider:

Faith Promise Update: Keep the congregation informed on the progress of the church in reaching its Faith Promise goal. Celebrate your progress and encourage continued support.

Field Reports: Read reports from the field concerning missions work that the church supports. This will demonstrate to the people that their giving is making a difference.

Dramas: Have the youth conduct a short drama with a theme about missions. A live drama can be a powerful visual presentation that reinforces the need for our involvement in the global harvest.

Keep the congregation connected to the global harvest.

Stories: Tell a real-life story about how the Gospel changed someone's life in a foreign country. Request these types of stories from your missionaries.

Prayer Request: You may receive a special or urgent prayer request from a missionary. Lead the congregation in prayer concerning the request.

Phone Call: Conduct a live phone call with one of your missionaries during the service. This should be prearranged with the missionary. The conversation should be amplified through the sound system so the whole congregation can hear. Conduct the call as a mini-interview discussing the well-being of the missionary family and their missions work. Hearing the actual voice of the missionary give a live report from the field is exciting, and it helps connect the missionary with the congregation in a more personal way.

Personal Testimonies: Have a member of your church give a personal testimony about how God supernaturally provided the finances for them to fulfill their Faith Promise commitment.

Music Specials: Have someone sing a special missions song or act out a missions scene to music.

Current Events: Share a special report on current events that are affecting the preaching of the Gospel in certain countries. Keep the people up to date on the state of the world so they are informed on how to pray for the global harvest.

Facts: State some interesting facts about a country where your church supports missions work. For example: *Did you realize that Niger, West Africa, ranks last in the world in providing education for their children? But this is an open door for the gospel! Even though Niger is ninety-eight percent Muslim, the people are so desperate for schooling for their children that they will pay money to send their children to school — even a Christian school. This is why we, as a church, are helping to build Christian schools in Niger. We have the opportunity to raise up a whole generation of new Christians in this country. Your giving is making it all possible!*

Videos: Short videos of different missions work prove to be very effective in connecting the congregation to the work in the field. Many missionaries now have the capability of providing fresh footage from their location. This can be done through email in most cases.

I recommend that you plan out the activities for your monthly Missions Sunday a year in advance. Start by identifying the date for your annual missions conference, then work out in both directions from there. Be creative and allow God to show you how to make Missions Sunday special. Your annual schedule may look something like this:

Plan out the activities for your monthly Missions Sundays a year in advance.

Launch the Congregation

Monthly Missions Sunday

January	Missionary speaker
February	Phone call from the field
March	A five-minute missions video
April	MISSIONS CONFERENCE
May	Prayer request from the field
June	Missionary speaker
July	Personal testimony concerning Faith Promise Giving
August	Field report
September	Missionary speaker
October	Music special about missions
November	Missions fact
December	Faith Promise update

E. Short-Term Missions Trips

Philosophy

Short-term missions trips... an important part of the church's missions strategy.

Short-term missions trips can be very effective and are an important part of the church's missions strategy. However, it is critical that the church isn't conducting short-term missions trips simply to provide an exciting activity for the youth or other members of the congregation. This type of motive tends to be self-serving and consumes large portions of the missions funds that could be used in a more effective way. A good philosophy to remember in order to produce fruitful, lasting results is to connect the short-term missions trip to a long-term field vision. This will help undergird and provide support to the on-going work of full-time missionaries, and it will guarantee that the work accomplished by the short-term missions team will receive adequate and effective follow-up.

For example, making converts on the streets and in parks has a limited purpose unless the converts are connected to an on-site, long-term ministry that can provide discipleship to the converts and nurturing in their new faith.

Strategy

The Missions Director will meet with the youth pastor and other selected church leaders to develop an annual plan for scheduled short-term missions trips organized from the church. Trips will be planned, organized, and implemented according to church protocol.

Protocol

1. The purpose of the short-term missions trip must be clearly identified. Example: A cruise on the Caribbean is normally not a missions trip, even though the participants leave their homeland and might have an opportunity to share the Gospel with someone on the trip.
2. The specific strategic mission to be achieved on the trip will be written so every participant can understand it thoroughly and can pray over it.
3. The church administrative protocols must be followed to help ensure an effective ministry within the trip's budget.
4. The participants are to raise their own finances to cover their cost of the trip. Exceptions are approved by the Missions Director.
5. After the trip, a summary report is to be submitted to the Missions Director by the trip's leader to help document the results and to help determine any follow-up action and the planning of possible subsequent trips.

Preparation

Preparation for short-term missions trips should be extensive. The trip's leader will meet with the group for not less than three months ahead of the trip. Areas of preparation will include:

Provide an offering for the host missionary.

Verify that all participants have passports.

1. Learn about the country and its Christian status. *Operation World* can serve as a good source.
2. Study the culture of the people who will be evangelized.
3. Know the background of the host(ess) missionary and information about his/her ministry.
4. Form prayer teams to pray for the trip daily.
5. Plan the trip (together with the participants if possible) by writing out the objectives and desired goals.
6. Submit the trip's plan to the MAT for approval.
7. Schedule the trip on the church's master calendar through the Missions Director.
8. Develop ministry strategies and train the trip's participants to accomplish these goals.
9. Distribute written information to help the participants learn simple phrases in the appropriate language.
10. Verify that all participants have passports with more than six months' time remaining from the date of departure from the United States or their home country so their visas will be approved.
11. Prepare a budget for financial obligations that will be incurred.
12. Raise adequate finances for the trip and some support for the host(ess) missionary.
13. Complete vaccination requirements according to the Country's Health Office.
14. Obtain short-term trip health and medical evacuation insurance.
15. A country safety briefing will be given by the trip's leader.
16. A country and ministry team orientation will be given by the host(ess) missionary when the short-term missions trip participants arrive.
17. Motivate the participants for full-time missionary service.
18. Document the trip with video, photos, etc. to share with the church.

LAUNCH THE CONGREGATION
DISCUSSION QUESTIONS:

Why is it important to have a strategy to get missions into the DNA of every department of the church?

Did you understand the biblical basis for the "Faith Giving" concept from 2 Corinthians 8:3?

IMPLEMENTATION PROCESS

7

*By following a series of action steps,
you can systematically implement all the key components
that are necessary in building a powerful
and effective missions church.*

A. Using the Quick Reference Sheet

Now that you have completed reading the *Global Pathway* manual, how do you implement the training in your church? Where do you start? How do you put into action all the components taught in the manual? The Quick Reference Sheet (Appendix G) provides you a step-by-step process on how to implement the training.

- **Useful Features:**

On the far left-hand column of the Quick Reference Sheet, there are eleven Action Steps listed. Each Action Step should be implemented in the order presented, because each step lays the foundation for the implementation of the next step. If the church has already implemented some of these steps before receiving the *Global Pathway* training, that is no problem. You can simply work what already exists into the Action Steps process.

On the center column of the Quick Reference Sheet, page numbers are given locating where each Action Step is taught in the manual. This gives you the ability to refer back to the helpful information as needed.

In the far right-hand column, each Action Step has a blank for you to write in a target date identifying when you want each step completed. By setting a target date, you help eliminate procrastination, and you keep the implementation process moving forward.

- **Special Pointer:**

In a normal situation, Action Steps 1–4 will require the active leadership and involvement of the pastor. By Action Step 5, the pastor will take on a more visionary, oversight role. Most of the workload will be turned over to the Missions Director and the Missions Advancement Team.

B. Action Steps – Descriptions

1. Read the manual

Refamiliarize yourself with the information and tools that the *Global Pathway* manual offers. Know that God has anointed your church to be a powerful instrument in impacting the world with the Good News.

2. Prepare Your Theological Presentation Regarding the Biblical Basis for Missions

Study chapters 1 and 2 to obtain a greater understanding of the Kingdom of God and The Great Commandment and Great Commission where you can internalize the passion and theology to lead a discussion. This will be used when sharing with your Core leaders and congregation.

3. Envision your Core leaders

Gather your Core leaders together for a special meeting. Share your passion for missions and explain how God has called every church to be a strong missions church. Cover the Five Areas listed under "Envision the Core."

4. **Create a Missions Advancement Team**

   This will give the church a team of people that will help develop and implement missions. Appoint a Missions Director to lead the Missions Advancement Team.

5. **Write a Missions Plan**

   This should be the first assignment for the Missions Advancement Team. A complete blueprint for writing a Missions Plan is in your manual. Modify the blueprint to match the church's vision for missions.

6. **Schedule a *Steps To The Mission Field* Workshop**

   Steps To The Mission Field is a supplement training designed to follow the *Global Pathway* training and initial implementation. The *Global Pathway* training sets up the church to be a strong missions church. *Steps To The Mission Field* helps the church create an established process for those in the congregation who want to become full-time, cross-cultural missionaries.

7. **Formulate an Annual Missions Calendar**

   Determine what organized missions activities the church wants to schedule for the coming year. Submit it to the church's leadership to be incorporated into the church's master calendar.

8. **Create a Missions Budget**

   Open a special account for missions that is separate from the church's general account. Formulate a strategy to develop the four income streams presented in the manual.

9. **Activate participation in missions in every department of the church**

Every part of the church should be involved in missions in the areas of envisioning, mobilizing, training, and serving. Each department is to come up with their own plan to accomplish this using the Departmental Missions Activation Form in the Appendix section of the manual. The Missions Advancement Team can assist each department develop their plan.

10. **Conduct an Annual Missions Conference**

This is one of the primary responsibilities of the Missions Advancement Team. Plan at least six months in advance of the conference date. Follow the pastor's guide on what to do in the four Sunday services leading up to the conference. Get as many members of your congregation involved with the conference as possible. Use the tools in the Appendix section pertaining to missions conferences. The Faith Promise Giving Service is the main component of the missions conference. Schedule a missions speaker who understands the Faith Promise Giving concept.

11. **Establish a monthly Missions Sunday**

This will help you maintain the momentum you created through the missions conference. Schedule the Missions Sunday on the same week each month. Have some type of special five-to-ten-minute missions presentation. Take a special offering for missions and encourage the people to stay faithful to their monthly commitment and their faith commitment.

C. Create a Missions Budget

Every church should have a financial account for the missions program that is separate from the church's general account. By setting up an account for missions, the church is taking a step of faith that missions funds are coming.

To help provide the necessary funds to support missionaries and conduct missions projects, here are four possible streams of income that any church can create:

1. **Ten percent of the general budget**

   Take ten percent of all monies that come into the general fund of the church and designate it for the missions program. This will serve as a powerful statement to the church and a powerful statement to God concerning the church's commitment to the global harvest. For some churches, the ten percent simply has served only as a starting point with the intention of increasing the percentage as the Lord provides.

   In an economically depressed part of the Ukraine, one Ukrainian church started giving a percentage of the church's overall income to missions, even though it was a tremendous sacrifice in the beginning. And although the economy of their country has not improved, the church has prospered. Today, this church gives twenty-five percent of the church's income to missions.

2. **Monthly Commitments**

   These are the monthly commitments that the families in the church made at the annual missions conferences. These commitments will generate new income into the account for missions every month.

3. **Faith Promises**

   By teaching the congregation the Faith Promise Concept and incorporating it into the annual missions conference, the people are learning to use their faith to believe in new finances for the missions budget from unknown resources.

4. **Special Fundraising Activities**

These are specially organized activities for the purpose of raising funds for the missions budget or for special missions projects. These activities may include bake sales, car washes, children's giving contests, auctions, and so on.

APPENDIX A

ANNUAL MISSIONS BUDGET SHEET
WORKSHEET FOR _____
(YEAR)

WORLD MISSIONS

Missionaries	Now Giving	Projected Giving
Missions Conference Fund		
Visiting Missionaries Fund		
Senders Fund (To assist missionary candidates)		
Christmas and Special Offerings for Missionaries		
Missions Agencies		
Special Projects Fund		

LOCAL MISSIONS

Missionaries	Now Giving	Projected Giving

APPENDIX B

DEPARTMENTAL MISSIONS ACTIVATION FORM

Missions should be like a thread that runs through every part of the church, because missions is not just a program in the church, but it is the purpose of the church! It serves as a unifying force that brings every department of the church together for a common purpose—the Great Commission. For this reason, every department head should determine how to incorporate missions into the DNA of their department. This planning sheet will help you make that process easier.

Four Areas of Activation:

Envision: How will you instill a vision for the global harvest in the _____ Department?

_____
_____
_____
_____

Mobilize: How will you mobilize the _____ Department into Great Commission ministry?

_____
_____
_____
_____

Train: How will you train the _____ Department to be knowledgeable and effective in Great Commission ministry?

_____
_____
_____
_____

Serve: How will the _____ Department serve the missions program of the church?

_____
_____
_____
_____

(Please return to the Missions Director)

APPENDIX C

MISSIONS CONFERENCE PLANNER WORKSHEET FOR _____
(YEAR)

8 MONTHS:

❏ Appoint the Missions Advancement Team (MAT) to coordinate the conference.

Chairperson (Missions Director):_____

❏ Set dates for the conference.

Our conference will consist of the following:

Type of Service	Date	Speaker

❏ Confirm the Speaker(s).

Service/Event	Speaker
Faith Promise Service	
Saturday Evening Banquet	
Sunday Evening Service	

4 MONTHS:

❏ Announce conference dates.
❏ Appoint other teams:

Appendix C

155

Decorations

Chairperson	
Additional Team Members	

Projects

Chairperson	
Additional Team Members	

Hospitality (For speakers)

Chairperson	
Additional Team Members	

Banquet

Chairperson	
Additional Team Members	

Conference Activities for Children

Chairperson	
Additional Team Members	

Conference Activities for Youth

Chairperson	
Additional Team Members	

Advertising

Chairperson	
Additional Team Members	

Prayer

Chairperson	
Additional Team Members	

Ushers and Tabulators

Chairperson	
Additional Team Members	

❏ Meet with all team members and church leaders. Explain in detail the Faith Promise Plan.

❏ Request letters, audio tapes, or video clips from the missionaries that you support.

3 MONTHS:

- ❏ Announce conference dates.
- ❏ Order conference materials.
- ❏ Request prayer for the conference.
- ❏ Meet with various teams to evaluate progress.

2 MONTHS:

- ❏ Announce conference dates.
- ❏ Activate prayer groups.
- ❏ Request prayer for the conference.
- ❏ Secure photos and biographies from the speaker(s).

1 MONTH:

- ❏ Promote the conference, including your Faith Promise Goal.
- ❏ Confirm that Faith Promise Cards are prepared.
- ❏ Reserve motel accommodations for your speaker(s).
- ❏ Include missions-related information in the bulletin.
- ❏ Meet with various team members for their reports.
- ❏ Make arrangements with children, youth, and Sunday School teachers for a missions emphasis during class time on Faith Promise Sunday.

3 WEEKS:

- ☐ Promote the conference with a skit.

- ☐ Share the Faith Promise Goal.

- ☐ Include missions' literature in the bulletin.

2 WEEKS:

- ☐ Promote the conference using the youth in a skit.

- ☐ Submit advertising.

- ☐ Announce special prayer meeting for next week.

- ☐ Meet with various team members for last-minute reports.

- ☐ Print the schedule for the conference in the bulletin.

- ☐ Prepare a sermon that emphasizes missions for next Sunday.

1 WEEK:

- ☐ Promote the conference in detail.

- ☐ Announce special prayer meeting for this week.

- ☐ Conduct a special prayer meeting.

- ☐ As pastor, preach a sermon that emphasizes missions.

- ☐ Decorate the church, using theme materials.

- ☐ Prepare a special missions conference bulletin with a thumbnail sketch of each missionary supported, the church's present missions budget, and the proposed missions budget.

Appendix C

APPENDIX D

MISSIONS CONFERENCE BUDGET WORKSHEET FOR _____
(YEAR)

Item	Estimate of your Expenditures:
Telephone	$
Advertising	
Newspaper	$
Radio	$
Television	$
Printing	
Bulletins	$
Other	$
Promotional	
Flags	$
Posters	$
Displays	$
Banquet	
Hall Rental	$
Food	$
Expenses for Speakers	
Food	$
Motel (_____days at $_____ per day)	$

Travel (Mileage: #_____ x standard mileage rate $0.____ = _____)
       OR
    (Air fare)
	$

Offering if missionary is speaking	$
Honorarium for Banquet	$
Honorarium for Sunday Morning Service	$
Honorarium for Sunday Evening Service	$
Miscellaneous Expenses	$
TOTAL	$

APPENDIX F

(Text for Faith Promise Card)

Faith Promise for Missions (Put Logo Here)

"For I testify that according to their ability and beyond their ability, they gave of their own accord..." 2 Corinthians 8:3

From known resources, I make a monthly commitment to the church missions program in the amount of $_____.

As the Lord provides, I make a faith promise to the church missions program in the amount of $_____

Name: _____

Address: _____

_____

APPENDIX G

GLOBAL PATHWAY

Quick Reference

Action Steps	Manual Reference	Timeline
1. Read the Manual	Pages 1–165	_____
2. Prepare Your Theological Presentation Regarding the Biblical Basis for Missions	Pages 3–44	_____
3. Envision your Core Leaders	Pages 65–78	_____
4. Create a MAT with a Missions Director	Pages 75–78, 91–96	_____
5. Write a Missions Plan	Pages 79, 85–113	_____
6. Schedule a "Steps to the Mission Field" Workshop	Page 147 *Steps* training manual	_____
7. Formulate an Annual Missions Calendar	Pages 82, 147	_____
8. Create a Missions Budget	Pages 148–151	_____
9. Activate Participation in Missions in Every Department of the Church	Pages 115–116, 148, 153–154	_____
10. Conduct an Annual Missions Conference	Pages 116–134, 148, 155–159, 163–165	_____
11. Establish a Monthly Missions Sunday	Pages 137–140	_____

GLOBAL PATHWAY EMPOWERS YOUR CHURCH TO CREATE
A COMPREHENSIVE APPROACH TO MISSIONS